101 ways to enjoy the MOSAIC

Creating a Diverse Community Right in Your Own Backyard

SKOT WELCH

Foreword by Michael C. Hyter

ISBN:978-1-62134-240-3

For Barbara, Brandon, Brooks and a host of amazing relatives and friends who continue to love and encourage me to make a difference. I love you.

Foreword

Throughout my career, and my life, I've been committed to helping others increase their contribution, both professionally and personally. I've learned along the way that leveraging the differences among people is the key to success. For example, in the corporate world, embracing diversity reduces barriers and empowers each employee to use all his or her talents fully to the benefit of the company—and it means that the company can serve each of their diverse consumer segments with sensitivity. As our world has become more and more global, cultural competence becomes more and more a driving force.

I built a diversity, inclusion, and talent development consulting company to help companies maximize the benefits of diversity. What started out as a training company eventually evolved into a consulting firm that has supported the development of business and cultural leaders around the world. A friend of mine introduced me to Skot Welch a few years ago because he felt since we were in a similar business we ought to know each other.

I remember our first meeting vividly. Skot and I agreed to meet for lunch in Chicago. Three hours later, though we had set aside only ninety minutes for our meeting, we were still talking.

Skot Welch, as an individual as well as through his firm Global Bridgebuilders, has been making a huge difference in the cultural competence abilities of clients worldwide for years. I am so excited to see that he's now written a book that speaks to how each of us can access and improve our own cultural competence.

Skot has captured the key ideas and approaches of cultural competencies and distilled them into practical, actionable steps anyone can take to find commonality with—as well as greater appreciation for differences among—our neighbors, and other would-be friends. I appreciate how Skot understands that all human beings are born naturally curious, but we tend to settle into a state of homogeneous comfort; in this book he draws a road map that can teach us how to break out of that rut and thrive.

This book stands out from others on the topic because it's motivational, and because it provides easy, step-by-step activities for real-time application—and because it's fun!

If you'd like to be able to not just celebrate diversity, but to navigate cultural nuances and differences effectively in a way that allows you to be successful in our fast-paced, ever smaller world, this is the book for you.

Michael C. Hyter
Managing Director
Korn Ferry

Contents

Way 1

Break Bread

IN HIS BOOK *MAKING ROOM FOR LIFE*, RANDY FRAZEE WROTE: "THE DINNER TABLE IS THE HEART OF COMMUNITY." THE SIMPLICITY AND TRUTH OF THIS STATEMENT RESONATES PROFOUNDLY. THE DINNER TABLE IS WHERE YOU LET YOUR GUARD DOWN, TAKE OFF YOUR 'GAME FACE' AND JUST RELAX. RECENTLY, MY WIFE AND I HAD DINNER WITH SOME NEW FRIENDS—THE HUSBAND IS FROM GREECE. AS WE SAT AT THEIR DINNER TABLE, EATING SOUVLAKI AND OTHER GREEK TREATS, THE CONVERSATION FLOWED EVER MORE EASILY. WE SHARED BOTH OUR DIFFERENCES AND WHAT WE HAD IN COMMON. BEFORE WE KNEW IT, WE HAD BEEN AT THE TABLE FOR FOUR HOURS. THE RICHNESS OF THE FOOD AND FELLOWSHIP CHASED THE TIME AWAY.

One of the most amazing ways to connect with someone who is different than you is to have dinner with him/her. The conversation, the gestures, the humanity that is shared is a powerful way to destroy myths, eliminate misunderstandings, and build lasting friendships.

Invite someone over to your house for dinner who has a different ethnic, cultural, and/or religious background than you. Prepare a meal that shows off your own culture with love and pride—whether that's souvlaki, samosa, fried green tomatoes, or spaghetti and meatballs—and let a great meal and great conversation begin.

Way 2
Celebrate

ONE OF THE RICHEST WAYS TO LEARN ABOUT A CULTURE IS TO BE A PART OF THAT CULTURE'S CELEBRATIONS. ETHNIC FESTIVALS ARE A WONDERFUL WAY TO ENJOY AND ENGAGE THE CULTURE. FROM THE MUSIC TO THE TRADITIONAL COSTUMES, FROM THE FOOD TO THE FELLOWSHIP, EVENTS OF THIS TYPE ARE BOTH EDUCATIONAL AND ENJOYABLE—AND, OFTEN, FREE!

"But Skot, you might say, I may be the only Black/White/Irish/Italian/Chinese/Native American person there!"

My answer is: So? This is a great opportunity for you to immerse yourself beyond your comfort zone.

For my own part, I really enjoy going to various ethnic festivals because they do stretch me. You know as well as I do that there is absolutely zero growth inside of your comfort zone. All growth is outside of it. Think of all the stereotypes and myths that have not only stood the test of time but have been perpetuated. Why? Because many of us live fairly "vertical" lives within our own group of people who think, look, and act very similarly to us. Instead, try living a little more "horizontally"—your circles transcending and traversing the varied cultural terrain. Yes, it may be uncomfortable at first, but I can promise you that you'll be all the richer for it.

★ ★

You can experience Chinese New Year or Filipino Independence Day or a Ramadan festival without even leaving the country, and often without even leaving your own geographical region. Check out your local event listings.

★ ★

Way 3

Tunage

IT HAS BEEN MY EXPERIENCE THAT THE THREE MOST EFFECTIVE WAYS CULTURES SHARE THEIR BEAUTY AND RICHNESS IS BY FOOD, VISUAL ART, AND MUSIC. ME, PERSONALLY—I'M PARTIAL TO MUSIC. YOU CAN TELL A LOT ABOUT A PERSON BY WHAT'S ON THEIR IPOD AND IF YOU WERE TO EVER TAKE A LOOK THROUGH MINE YOU WOULD FIND ALL SORTS OF MUSIC FROM ALL AROUND THE WORLD. BUT DON'T JUST TAKE MY WORD FOR IT—ASK ANY CULTURAL ENTHUSIAST AND YOU'LL FIND THAT MUSIC PLAYS A VERY IMPORTANT ROLE IN HER LIFE.

That's because music is, truly—all clichés aside—the universal language. The heart of a people comes through so clearly when you hear their music, and you can connect more intimately with universal emotions—the joy, anguish, longing, and love—that all people everywhere share but that can best be articulated through melody.

This emotional connection isn't limited to cultures, either, but can cross generational lines as well. I heard my daughter tell a friend that there are certain jazz songs her mom and I enjoy so much, and so often, that she knows the entire melody by heart and can sing it back, note for note. How cool is that?

Go out and buy some tunes from another country, culture, or even generation. Don't limit yourself—choose a genre you wouldn't normally listen to or, if you normally sing along with the lyrics, download or pick up an instrumental CD. It may take a while, but there's a good chance it will grow on you.

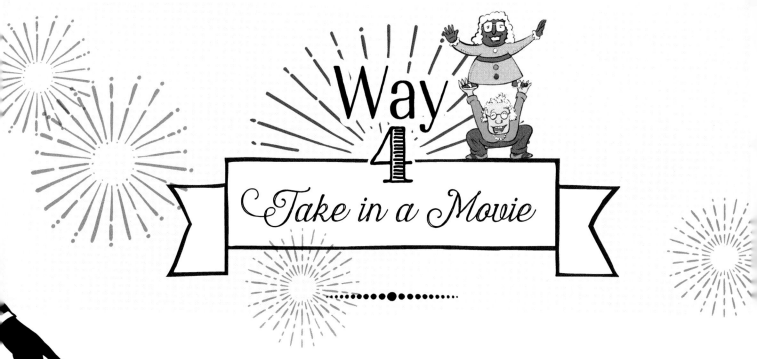

Way 4

Take in a Movie

ONE SURE WAY TO GET TO KNOW MORE ABOUT A CULTURE IS TO WATCH SOME OF THEIR FILMS. FILMS FROM OTHER COUNTRIES DO SUCH A GREAT JOB PROVIDING INSIGHT INTO THE NUANCES OF A CULTURE. YOU CAN'T WATCH *CINEMA PARADISO* AND COME AWAY WITHOUT A DEEPER UNDERSTANDING OF THE CULTURE'S UNDERSTANDING OF ITS OWN HISTORY, OR *SEVEN SAMURAI* WITHOUT A DEEPENING APPRECIATION FOR JAPAN'S TRADITION OF ARTISANSHIP. TO WATCH LOVE AND FEAR, LOYALTY AND BETRAYAL, FAMILY RELATIONSHIPS AND FRIENDSHIPS PLAY OUT THROUGH THE EYES OF SOMEONE WHO HAS A TOTALLY DIFFERENT VIEW OF THE WORLD THAN YOU DO—WELL, IT CAN TOTALLY OPEN UP YOUR OWN WORLDVIEW.

I believe so strongly in the power of film that I started a global youth film festival, The Mosaic Film Experience (*www.mosaicfilmexperience.com*) that focuses on giving high school and college students an opportunity to share their stories their way. It's so uplifting to receive literally hundreds of submissions from all around the world from our young people. They share such keen insights and are so articulate in their views that it is impossible not to be encouraged by their storytelling ability.

The reason we target young people? Because the sooner we understand that the world is bigger than the block on which we live, the sooner we truly start living. Film is a great way to travel the world, and to tell your story to the world, when, like many young people, your budget is too tight to actually do a whole lot of traveling!

Watch a movie about another culture—maybe even one with subtitles! Here's just one list of top foreign films to get you started: *www.imdb.com/list/ls000107883/*

Way 5
"Sprechen Sie Deutsch?"

IALWAYS ENJOY SPENDING TIME IN THE MIDST OF FOLKS WHILE THEY ARE SPEAKING DIFFERENT LANGUAGES. I KNOW IT'S WEIRD; BEING SURROUNDED BY A LANGUAGE THEY DON'T UNDERSTAND MAKES MOST PEOPLE NERVOUS, BUT IT'S INTRIGUING TO ME. AND WHILE THAT'S FUN, IT'S MORE FUN TO CONVERSE (OR AT LEAST TRY TO CONVERSE) IN ANOTHER LANGUAGE. I WAS AN ARMY BRAT AND ONE OF THE KEY CHAPTERS IN MY LIFE WAS LIVING IN A SMALL VILLAGE NEAR SEOUL, KOREA—NOT ON THE MILITARY BASE, BUT IN THE VILLAGE LIKE EVERYONE ELSE. I LEARNED JUST ENOUGH KOREAN TO MAKE ME, AS THEY SAY, DANGEROUS. BUT I WAS FLUENT ENOUGH TO BE INSPIRED TO LEARN TO BE DANGEROUS IN GERMAN TOO.

Globalization is here to stay. That is, we now live in a global community. Part of living in this new reality is taking at least a shot at becoming a more fluent global citizen by diving into a new language. From a professional development standpoint, it will definitely make you more marketable. Even learning just a few key words and phrases before you travel to your destination will go a long way in how the locals view you—you will have shown your respect for the country you are visiting by your willingness to step up and into new territory in a cultural as well as a geographical sense. It also makes it so much less stressful when you need a bathroom to be able to simply ask where the bathroom is instead of having to pantomime your distress.

★★★★★★★★★★★★★★★★★★★★★★★★★★★★

Sign up for (and complete) a foreign language class. Rosetta Stone is an excellent option for home study (*www.rosettastone.com*). If you don't have a lot of wiggle room in your schedule, or the disposable income to invest in a standard language class, try learning a language through the web site Duolingo (*www.duolingo.com*)—each lesson is short, the method they use wildly effective, and the service is totally free!

Way 6

Globetrot

I WAS SURPRISED TO FIND OUT HOW MANY COUNTRIES THERE ARE IN THE WORLD—ABOUT 196! I THOUGHT I WAS WELL TRAVELED ONLY TO FIND OUT THAT I'VE JUST BARELY SCRATCHED THE SURFACE. "SKOT," I MUTTERED TO MYSELF, "YOU REALLY NEED TO GET OUT MORE."

I believe with all my heart that one of the most important things that a parent can pass on to his or her children is a global mindset. To not take that seriously is to stunt their intellectual growth as global citizens. And if you can't currently take your kids to visit another country and culture, take them to an ethnic neighborhood in your own city and let them watch the street scene and taste the food. At the very least, get them on the Internet where they can explore and learn.

I am a firm believer in the notion that many of the problems we face as a global society is that we don't spend enough time with each other asking the right questions. Questions like: What's your story? Where are you from? What's important to you? How can I help? These are just a few questions that can open up very "big rooms" of conversation for learning to take place. When you meet people in their own neighborhoods, and share a conversation based around some of the fundamental questions, you will notice how very much all people have in common. Most human beings, after all, want the same things: to make a difference, to be happy, to live a life of purpose.

Moreover, I will tell you that tomorrow's leaders will be those people with a sense of what makes the various cultures around the world tick. Knowing this, here's a statistic that should scare you: in comparison to other countries of its size, the U.S. ranked dead last in terms of the number of its citizens who hold passports. Not good. The only way to change that is to get yours—and to make sure your kids have theirs.

Get your passport! Make a family event out of going out to have your passport photos taken.

Way 7

Thank a Veteran

FOR ALL THE "SUPPORT OUR TROOPS" BUMPER STICKERS WE SEE THE HIGHWAY AND POLITICAL PLATITUDES WE HEAR IN ELECTION SEASONS, WE OFTEN FORGET THAT BEING LOYAL TO THE MEN AND WOMEN WHO SERVE OUR COUNTRY INCLUDES REMEMBERING THEM EVEN WHEN THEY ARE NO LONGER IN ACTIVE SERVICE. THERE IS NO GREATER LOVE THAN WHEN ONE LAYS DOWN ONE'S LIFE FOR A FRIEND, BUT WHAT ABOUT SACRIFICING YOURSELF AND EVEN YOUR LIFE FOR PEOPLE YOU'VE NEVER MET? THIS IS WHAT VETERANS HAVE DONE.

What strikes my heart with gladness is when I listen to a veteran speak about what they have actually fought for—what moved them to sign up for the hard job of protecting and serving, and sustained them while they did it. You won't hear a veteran mouthing platitudes! What you will hear, time after time, is that what they were fighting for was to protect the ideals of our nation. Their commitment was not to safeguard a particular ethnic group or gender orientation or religion—their commitment was to keep America free for all people.

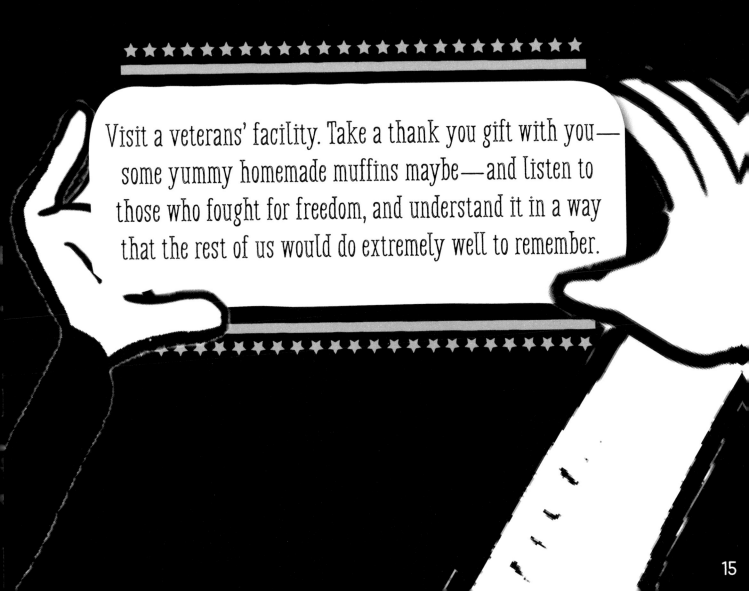

Visit a veterans' facility. Take a thank you gift with you— some yummy homemade muffins maybe—and listen to those who fought for freedom, and understand it in a way that the rest of us would do extremely well to remember.

Way 8
What's for Dinner?

A COUPLE OF SUMMERS AGO, MY FAMILY AND I HAD THE PLEASURE OF TOURING EUROPE. AS PART OF THE FUN, WE SIGNED UP FOR A COOKING CLASS FROM A FAMOUS ITALIAN CHEF. THE CLASS TOOK PLACE IN THE CHEF'S APARTMENT IN ROME WITH A TOTAL OF ABOUT TEN PEOPLE FROM DIFFERENT PARTS OF THE WORLD. HE PUT US TO WORK PREPARING THE MEAL, ALL FIVE COURSES, STARTING WITH A TOUR OF THE LOCAL MARKET TO BUY ALL OF THE INGREDIENTS. NONE OF US STUDENT CHEFS HAD MUCH EXPERIENCE COOKING REAL ITALIAN FOOD (OR SPEAKING ITALIAN, FOR THAT MATTER!) AND EACH OF US MADE MANY MISTAKES DURING THE COURSE OF OUR FEW HOURS IN THE CHEF'S KITCHEN. WE STUDENTS, HOWEVER, WERE PERSISTENT AND POSITIVE, AND THE CHEF WAS SO PATIENT WITH US; AND, AT THE END OF THE DAY, WE HAD AN AMAZING MEAL.

Had we let the chef prepare the meal for us, it would have been perfect. But we would not have learned anything at all about Italian cooking, and it would not have been nearly such a special experience.

Invite a few friends to gather at your house for dinner, and their ticket for admission is that they have to prepare a dish to pass around from a country that is not their own. Share in the food, and educate each other on the dish that you prepared and the country in which it originated. Sure, the dish that you prepare may not be perfect, especially if it's the first time you're trying your hand at eggrolls or paella, but as much as this is about food, this is also about building community while stretching yourself. Bon Appetit!

Way 9
Sister to Sister

IN CASE YOU JUST JOINED THE PROGRAM ALREADY IN PROGRESS—OUR WORLD HAS GONE GLOBAL. THE PRODUCTS AND SERVICES WE USE—AS WELL AS WE OURSELVES—TRAVEL THE SEAS MORE EFFICIENTLY AND FASTER THAN EVER BEFORE, AND OFTEN AT WILL.

One of efforts that I really appreciate is the Sister City program (*sister-cities.org*). This program isn't new—it was founded in 1956 by President Dwight D. Eisenhower—and it now connects "tens of thousands of citizen diplomats and volunteers in 545 communities with over 2,100 partnerships in 145 countries on six continents..." (*sister-cities.org/about-sister-cities-international*). My city—Grand Rapids, Michigan—has several sister cities and, in my experience, one of the prominent benefits of this initiative is that it opens doors for the leaders of the cities to exchange ideas and explore opportunities for the communities to do business together.

Another opportunity that a Sister City program affords is the chance for the student populations in both communities to build lifelong friendships. And the more adept our young people become in working across cultures, the smaller and more tangible our global village becomes.

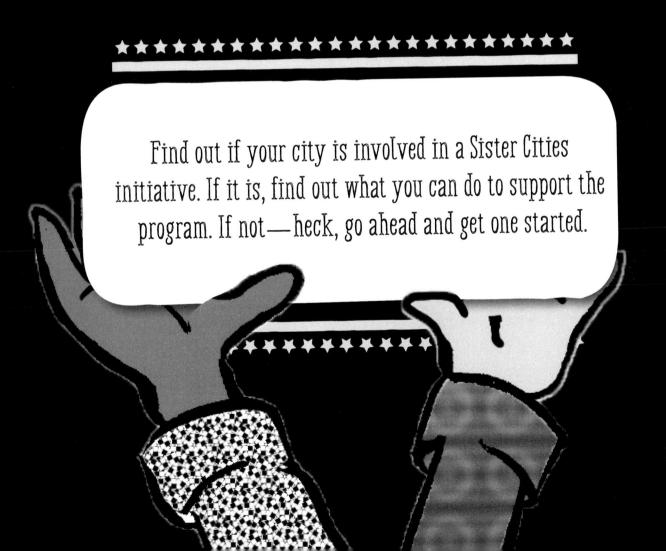

Find out if your city is involved in a Sister Cities initiative. If it is, find out what you can do to support the program. If not—heck, go ahead and get one started.

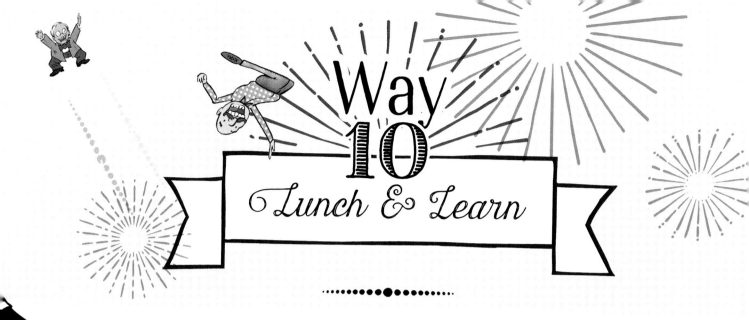

Way 10
Lunch & Learn

SN'T IT FUNNY HOW WE TALK ABOUT TRYING SOMETHING NEW OR GOING TO A NEW PLACE BUT SO FEW OF US REALLY DO EITHER? WE SAY: WOULDN'T IT BE GREAT TO GO TO THAT NATIVE AMERICAN HARVEST FESTIVAL IN NEW MEXICO THIS FALL? DOESN'T IT SOUND FUN AND INTERESTING? BUT WHEN IT COMES DOWN TO IT, COORDINATING THE FAMILY'S SCHEDULE, AND JUMPING IN THE CAR FOR THE DRIVE OR BUYING PLANE TICKETS FOR THE FLIGHT, AND BOOKING THE ROOMS—WELL, A GOOD INTENTION FOR A FUN AND EDUCATIONAL FAMILY MINI-VACATION FIZZLES. SO LET'S KEEP IT SIMPLE, SHALL WE? ASK SOMEONE WHO IS DIFFERENT FROM YOU TO HAVE LUNCH. I MEAN, WE ALL HAVE TO EAT, AND MOST OF US EAT LUNCH EVERY DAY—ASK SOMEONE WHO MIGHT NOT EVER, IN THE NORMAL COURSE OF EVENTS, SHARE THE MEAL WITH YOU. MY BET IS THAT YOU'LL FIND OUT A LOT ABOUT THE PERSON JUST BY MAKING

LUNCH ARRANGEMENTS. AT THE VERY LEAST YOU'LL FIND OUT IF SHE LIKES KIMCHI OR IF HE PREFERS TO CHOW DOWN ON SOME GOOD STREET FOOD ON A BENCH IN THE LOCAL PARK.

And then? Talk. Just talk. The man who sits in the cubicle three desks down from yours? Ask him how he came to be working for the company that employs you both. The woman who is buying that great yarn at the yarn shop? Ask her how she came to enjoy knitting as much as you do. The teenager who mows your lawn? Take a glass of iced tea and some turkey sandwiches outside when she's done with the work and ask her what grade she's in in school, what her hobbies are, if she plays sports, if she likes working outdoors.

What do you already have in common with all the people I've just used as examples? You already know them! Now, get to know them a little better—find out about their hobbies and, before you know it, you'll be talking with them about their dreams and deeper concerns.

★ ★

Make a lunch date with someone who doesn't expect the invitation. I know this might be uncomfortable, initially, but this book is all about putting yourself in potentially uncomfortable situations—this is how we grow.

Way 11
Go Grocery Shopping

MY WIFE, BARBARA, AND I HAD THE OPPORTUNITY TO SPEND SOME TIME IN JAMAICA SOME YEARS AGO. WE REALLY CONNECTED WITH OUR HOUSEKEEPER AND SHE OFFERED TO PREPARE A MEAL FOR US. THIS WAS NOT A REQUIREMENT OF THE JOB BUT SOMETHING THAT SHE WANTED TO DO FROM THE GENEROSITY OF HER HEART. SHE TOOK US TO THE MARKET WITH HER TO BUY ALL OF THE MEAT AND THE VEGGIES—CUTS OF MEAT AND TYPES OF VEGETABLES THAT WEREN'T STOCKED IN OUR GROCERY STORE AT HOME! WHENEVER I THINK OF JAMAICA NOW, I REMEMBER THE SIGHTS, SMELLS AND SOUNDS AS WE MEANDERED THROUGH THE MARKETPLACE TO FIND THE CHOICEST MEATS AND VEGETABLES. AFTER OUR SHOPPING TRIP, OUR HOUSEKEEPER PREPARED THE FOOD WE'D BOUGHT AND WE HAPPILY ATE IT WHILE LOOKING OVER THE BAY. WE HAVE BROUGHT THAT TRADITION HOME WITH US AND LIKE PREPARING FOODS FROM DIFFERENT COUNTRIES. WELL, BARBARA DOES THAT—I DO THE EATING.

One of the quantifiable indicators of the diversity climate of a community is how many ethnic supermarkets and grocery stores it contains. Having this option is a wonderful asset in any community—how many of these assets do you have in your neighborhood? In your town? How many grocery shops that cater to your city's Asian, or Latino, or Middle Eastern populations?

Visit an ethnic food market. If the food of that culture is new to you, go online to identify particular dishes that appeal to you, and might be easiest to execute for a cook who's trying out that cuisine for the first time. Make a list and purchase the ingredients for your dinner, prepare it in the authentic way, and have some people over to share in the dish.

Way 12
Try on a New Pair of Shoes

HUMAN COMPASSION REQUIRES AN OPEN HEART AS WELL AS AN OPEN MIND. SOMETIMES, WE CAN GET SO IMMERSED IN OUR OWN CONCERNS THAT WE FORGET LIFE IS A FULL CONTACT SPORT, AND INTER-ACTION WITH OUR FELLOW HUMAN BEINGS IS REQUIRED IN ORDER TO PLAY. ONE OF THE MOST POWERFUL THINGS THAT ANY OF US CAN DO IS TO TAKE THE TIME TO UNDERSTAND MORE FULLY THE FOLKS WITH WHOM WE'RE PLAYING THIS WONDERFUL GAME OF LIFE.

I believe it is necessary to know a person's story in order to truly make a one-to-one connection with them. Agreeing with that person in every way may not ever happen, but it shouldn't need to in order for you to empathize with each other. But empathy is in short supply these days. That is likely because there is a lot more talking than listening going on—and unless we take the time to listen intentionally to each other we run the risk of leaving the next generation a society that is not only hard of hearing but hard of heart.

★ ★

Open up a newspaper or a tab on your computer and find a photo of another person who is different from you. Maybe it's a photo of someone who lives in an exotic place, or maybe it's someone who espouses politics that are the polar opposite of yours. Are they rich, or are they poor, or are they middle class? Are they healthy? Are their daily needs being met? How? How would you fare if you lived their daily life? Ask yourself what life events may have occurred in order for them to develop their worldview. Find out how a policy they championed actually helped people rather than dismissing their whole ideology out of partisanship.

Way 13

Moments in Mobility

IT MAY COME AS A SURPRISE TO YOU BUT THE LARGEST "PROTECTED CLASS" OF CITIZENS ARE THOSE WITH A VALIDATED PHYSICAL DISABILITY. PINNING DOWN AN EXACT NUMBER IS DIFFICULT, BECAUSE THE CENSUS BUREAU COLLECTS DATA THROUGH A NUMBER OF DIFFERENT SURVEYS, BUT THE ESTIMATE IS SOMEWHERE AROUND 51.2 MILLION AMERICANS, OR 18% OF THE TOTAL POPULATION.

For you business folks out there, can you say: Huge market segment with lots of buying power! What is even more interesting is that the differently-abled are at last becoming more visible—we are finally seeing more people with a physical disability in movies, television shows, and commercials. In my work, which focuses on *Innovation Through Inclusion*®, I am constantly both learning myself and striving to help other people "get it" when it comes to understanding how people with

...ilities are best able to function in a world that has been bu...

...abled people. For example, I have asked people who work in va...

...nizations how mobility friendly their workplace is and often ...

...knee-jerk response is that it is incredibly easy to move ar...

...eir environment. Unfortunately, this response almost inva...

...s from someone who doesn't have a physical disability. So, ho...

...d out what the answer to my question really is?

★ ★

Have a team of people in your company who do not have a physical disability use wheelchairs around the office and at home for forty-eight hours. When they've completed the experiment, have a discussion about the insights they've acquired, and how your workplace could be better prepared to welcome the differently-abled, and to leverage their skills and talents. Talk with your local disability advocate about the ideas this experiment generates.

Way 14
Pass It On

YES, WE'RE ALL BUSY AND HAVE PLENTY TO DO, BUT IN THE MIDST OF OUR BUSY LIVES WE NEED TO KEEP THIS TRUTH TOP-OF-MIND: THE ONLY THING THAT WILL LIVE ON AFTER WE'VE DEPARTED THIS EARTH IS WHAT WE LEAVE DEPOSITED IN THE LIVES OF OTHERS. I CAN'T THINK OF A BETTER WAY TO LIVE ON THAN TO DEPOSIT OUR ENERGY, KINDNESS, AND WISDOM WITH THE NEXT GENERATION.

Our children need us. And when I say "our" I am not talking only about the children who may biologically belong to us. Children in every community are raising themselves because their parents are absent, or working several jobs to make ends meet. Let's be very clear: It's not the fault of the children if their parents are poor, and it isn't their fault if their parents are neglectful either. It's easy for any of us to say this shouldn't be the case, or to bemoan that it happens. The much harder thing for us to do is to look in the mirror and, in the words of the amazing leader Mahatma Gandhi, be the change that we want to see in the world. We all know that parents should be there for their kids. We all know that kids shouldn't be raising kids. We all know that, ideally, every child born in this world comes home from the hospital to a financially and emotionally stable home life. But guess what? A lot of kids live in home situations that haven't yet met our ideal. Now what? Help anyway. Pass on all the good you can.

Volunteer at your local school, or Big Brother/Big Sister organization. Help a young person improve his reading skills. Take a young person out to a baseball game. Teach and tutor and mentor like your community's life depended on it—because it does, and so does yours, because we all know the way it will turn out if you do: two lives will be changed instead of one. You've got nothing to lose and everything to gain. Here's a great resource to inspire you: *www.teachforamerica.org.*

Way 15
Offering Thanks

I REMEMBER STUDYING WORLD RELIGIONS AS AN UNDERGRAD, AND HOW PROFOUNDLY THE CLASS OPENED MY EYES. OVER THE YEARS I HAVE FOUND THAT HAVING MY VIEWS CHALLENGED IS VERY HEALTHY—IT HELPS ME TO DISCOVER WHAT I TRULY BELIEVE IN, AND I AM THE STRONGER FOR IT.

When you speak with someone who has different beliefs than you—when you open yourself up to understanding their faith, and even go to a different faith service not to poke holes in their way of worship but to listen and learn—you put yourself into an extraordinary position. What you'll find is that in the midst of often very clear differences, there is so much that is in alignment in all faith traditions. The concepts of love, hope, charity, forgiveness, and the value of quiet contemplation infuse all of the major world religions. If you were to stand all of my friends from one end to the other—Christians, Muslims, Jews, Buddhists, and more—you would see those values reflected in all of those people, though we perform our worship in different ways, we love each other no less for it. Sometimes, when we discuss our religions together, we do find ourselves in disagreement, but we've committed to always come back to the table to work through and learn to appreciate our differences. It takes tenacity, heart, and maturity, but hey, who said it would be easy?

Attend a celebration or service of a
different religious tradition with a
curious mind and an open heart.

Way 16

Umoja

THERE ARE SO MANY AMAZING HOLIDAYS THAT VARIOUS CULTURES HAVE CONTRIBUTED TO OUR WORLD—CINCO DE MAYO; MARDI GRAS; THE SPRING FESTIVALS THAT CELEBRATE THE HARVEST, AND THE NEW YEAR, IN CHINA, KOREA, VIETNAM, AND OTHER ASIAN COUNTRIES. UMOJA, OR UNITY, IS THE FIRST OF THE SEVEN PRINCIPLES OF KWANZAA, AN AFRICAN-AMERICAN AND PAN-AFRICAN HOLIDAY THAT IS CELEBRATED FROM DECEMBER 26TH THROUGH JANUARY 1ST OF EACH YEAR. THE HOLIDAY, A TIME OF REFLECTION, APPRECIATION, AND REAFFIRMATION, CELEBRATES FAMILY, COMMUNITY, AND CULTURE. THOUGH ITS PRINCIPLES ARE NOT WIDELY KNOWN OUTSIDE OF THE AFRICAN COMMUNITY, I'M SURE THAT IF THEY WERE THEY WOULD SPEAK TO A MUCH BROADER CROSS SECTION OF THE POPULATION, AND MORE PEOPLE WOULD BE DRAWN INTO ITS CELEBRATION.

"But I'm not African," you might say. Well, actually, we all kind of are African—the bones of the oldest human in history, from which we all derive some part of our DNA, were found on the continent of... You guessed it! Africa!—but that's another conversation altogether. My point here is that when you look into what Kwanzaa is all about, you might find yourself wanting to incorporate some of its tenets into your life because the ideals contained in this tradition transcend culture: Unity, Self-Determination, Collective Work and Responsibility, Cooperative Economics, Purpose, Creativity and Faith. I mean, how could anyone have a problem embracing any of these? Harambee!

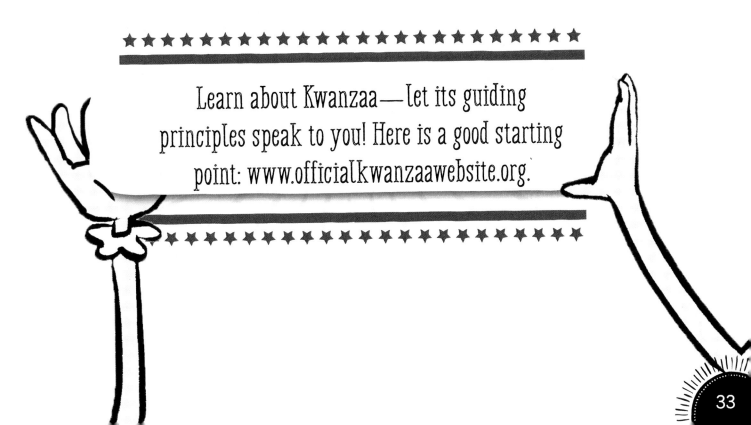

Learn about Kwanzaa—let its guiding principles speak to you! Here is a good starting point: www.officialkwanzaawebsite.org.

Way 17
Wisdom of the Elders

ONE OF OUR GREATEST, THOUGH TOO OFTEN OVERLOOKED GLOBAL TREASURES IS OUR ELDERLY. THEY POSSESS WISDOM FORGED THROUGH THE EXPERIENCE OF LIVED HISTORY, AND THE INSIGHTS THEY ARE CAPABLE OF PROVIDING CAN MAKE OUR OWN LIVES RICHER, MORE SATISFYING, AND LESS FRUSTRATING. YES, IN SOME INSTANCES, AND ESPECIALLY IN SOME COUNTRIES, THEY'RE RELEGATED TO PLACES OF ISOLATION—CONVALESCENT FACILITIES, RETIREMENT COMMUNITIES, OLD FOLKS HOMES—LIKE DIAMONDS HIDDEN FROM SIGHT.

I remember once in Europe, as a young man, spending time with a Norwegian war veteran in his senior citizens' home. I didn't speak any Norwegian at all, but I had a translator and my questions for my elder, in any case, were simple, boiling down to: Sir, tell me your story. Two

s later, he had become my new surrogate grandpa. His willin
hare his story, and the humanity of that story, connected us in
was so intimate. I was a global grandson rapt by an ageless
pped up in the flesh of a great man. I was forever changed aft
ting with this veteran. Indeed, I think this was a defining mo
ne in terms of knowing what I wanted to do with my life.

r seniors are our living history. They are our link to all the history
at humanity has learned in all that ancient time. Never make the m
lieving that you are "self-made". Every one of us stands on the sho
those who came before us—their advances and triumphs, as well a
s and mistakes. These great men and women paved the way for yo
and if we would take the time to listen to them, we would find tha
om makes for smoother travel for us youngsters.

★ ★

Make a date with your grandfather or grandmother, a great
aunt or uncle, or an elderly neighbor and simply ask them to
tell you their story. Then listen. If you aren't fortunate enough
to have elders in your life, volunteer at your local elder-care
facility. Even one afternoon a month will broaden your
understanding of the world, and your place in it.

Way 18

The Global Palate

FOOD IS ONE OF THE PRIMARY WAYS CULTURES COMMUNICATE WHO THEY ARE. THERE ARE FEW THINGS MORE DELIGHTFUL THAN GOING TO A RESTAURANT AND TASTING CUISINE THAT IS COMPLETELY NEW TO YOU. I CONSIDER MYSELF A PERSON WITH A FAIRLY BROAD PALETTE, CULTIVATED WAY BACK IN MY CHILDHOOD, WHEN I LIVED IN KOREA. MY MILITARY PARENTS MADE IT A POINT THAT OUR FAMILY ATE THE SAME FOOD AS THE FOLKS IN THE VILLAGE WHERE WE WERE STATIONED—IN KOREA, THAT MEANT KIMCHI, YAKIMANDO, BULGOGI!

One of the most flabbergasting experiences of my life happened when I was in Beijing, on a tour bus with some American MBA students. At lunchtime, the bus pulled up to the curb to let us all out so we could find a restaurant. Like Olympic sprinters, the students rushed off the bus and raced to two of the many eateries lining the street: Pizza Hut and McDonalds! When the young people got back to the bus, I had an earful for them: *You're in CHINA! Why would you even come to China if you didn't want to immerse yourself in the experience of it?* Suffice to say that the students never again opted for an American hamburger on our trip. That's because they went out of their comfort zone to try new taste sensations and, as a result, their palates were expanded. Once your palate is expanded it can never again be satisfied by the ordinary.

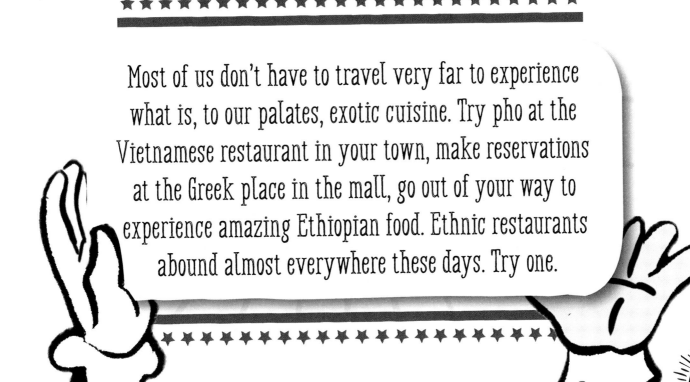

Most of us don't have to travel very far to experience what is, to our palates, exotic cuisine. Try pho at the Vietnamese restaurant in your town, make reservations at the Greek place in the mall, go out of your way to experience amazing Ethiopian food. Ethnic restaurants abound almost everywhere these days. Try one.

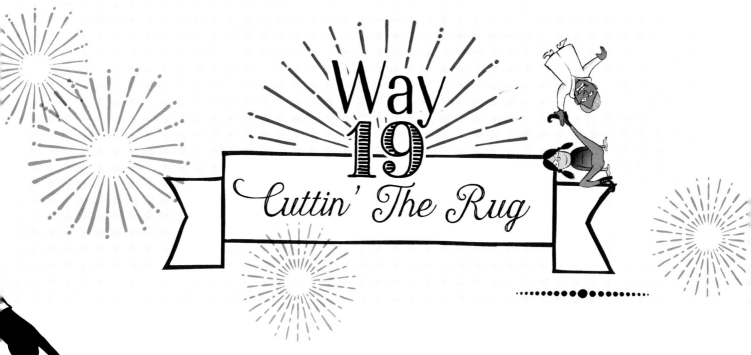

Way 19
Cuttin' The Rug

DANCING IS ONE OF THE MOST FUN AND EXUBERANT ACTIVITIES ON THE PLANET—AND ABSOLUTELY ANYONE CAN PARTICIPATE. THINK I'M EXAGGERATING? CHECK OUT THIS WHEELCHAIR DANCE COMPETITION AT *WWW.YOUTUBE.COM/WATCH?V=PCY2BR7MPVO*, OR ANY OF THE WONDERFUL VIDEOS OF ELDERLY FOLKS GETTING THEIR GROOVE ON HERE: *WWW.YOUTUBE.COM/WATCH?V=6Z3I9OULDAQ*.

Dance is also one of the most accessible cultural bridges you can imagine. I remember when Barbara and I were visiting some friends in Namibia and one evening they had multi-cultural night where various people would do dances and sing songs from their culture. I remember the folks from Angola got up and began to do a dance that was hundreds of years old. But guess what? It looked like the modern-day dance that we call The Hustle. It's all connected, folks. All connected.

Personally, I love to dance. I love to watch people dancing, and I love all different types of dance. But, whether I'm participating in the dance, or I'm attending a dance performance as a spectator, I do have my favorites—country line dancing and salsa. I appreciate the precision and passion that are the foundations of these beautiful art forms. You might prefer swing dancing, contra dancing, hip-hop dancing, belly dancing, the tango! Dance is, for me, the most high-spirited way to take part in the global festival going on all around us, every day.

Find a dance class in your area. Not only is it a great way to meet new people, learn about a different culture, and build community, it's also the most fun you'll ever have while staying in shape! Step out and try some sweet new dance steps—what have you got to lose other than, possibly, your dignity?

Way 20
Go Native

I AM ELATED BY HOW VARIOUS CULTURES ARE BEGINNING TO TELL THEIR OWN STORIES. NOVELISTS, CHOREOGRAPHERS, MOVIE MAKERS, MUSICIANS—ARTISTS FROM EVERY DISCIPLINE AND ALL ACROSS THE RAINBOW ARE ADDING COLORS AND CULTURES THAT HAVE LONG BEEN MISSING FROM WHAT WERE ONCE THE CLASSIC WESTERN CANONS. THIS TREND IS SOMETHING TO REALLY CELEBRATE, AND TO SUPPORT BY READING AND LISTENING AND VIEWING AS BROADLY AS THE BODIES OF WORK THEMSELVES.

I do, however, want to make the case for a culture that is too frequently overlooked when we discuss diversity: Native Americans. We often forget that Native Americans were the first true Americans. I believe that in order to understand America itself, we need to understand it in context, and that includes the struggles and triumphs of our Native American brothers and sisters. Their story is our story. Before anyone else got here—before Columbus "discovered" the place—Native Americans had already cultivated a rich and beautiful culture. I believe the more deeply we know and respect the traditions that first shaped our country, the more we, as new Americans, will learn about ourselves.

Read a novel by Leslie Marmon Silko or Sherman Alexie. Rent the movie *Smoke Signals*. Visit the National Museum of the American Indian in Washington, DC, or the Museum of the Institute of American Indian Arts in Santa Fe, New Mexico. Go out of your way to learn more about these great people who are the original Americans.

Way 21
Wasabi

LOVE HEAT. THAT IS, I PREFER MY FOOD HOT AND SPICY. I'VE NEVER MET A PEPPER I DIDN'T LIKE, OR A CUISINE THAT PUT ME OFF WITH ITS INTENSITY—A BLAZING VINDALOO OR SOME SZECHUAN FIRE, I WAS IN! I THOUGHT I'D EXPERIENCED EVERY SORT OF CULINARY HEAT—AND THEN I TRIED WASABI.

Years ago, I went out to lunch at a Japanese restaurant with a friend of mine. It was my first time trying sushi, and I went on a binge—it was delicious! Well, trying sushi for the first time wasn't enough of an adventure for me, so my friend and I decided to take it up to the next level. We used our chopsticks to swirl a large pinch of wasabi into our tiny dish of soy sauce, the pale green paste looked so harmless… But, wow!

Wasabi is made from the root of a Japanese plant that is from the same family as horseradish and mustard. It doesn't burn your tongue, but emits vapors that sort of sneak attack your whole sinus cavity. It isn't your taste buds that feel the heat; rather it's your brain that feels wrapped in clean, fresh, almost unbearable warmth. What a rush! Because of its fierce punch, you may end up making some faces you've never made and sounds you've never uttered when you try it for the first time. Don't say I didn't warn you!

Try sushi. For those of you who balk at the idea of eating raw fish, start with something a bit more tame, like a California roll—which contains only cooked crab as its seafood—and work your way up. If you're really feeling daring, try some wasabi with it.

Way 22
Enduring Legacy

AS A YOUNG MAN I HAD THE OPPORTUNITY TO VISIT DACHAU, ONE OF THE FIRST NAZI CONCENTRATION CAMPS LOCATED JUST OUTSIDE OF MUNICH, GERMANY. I WAS THERE WITH THE GROUP OF MUSICAL AMBASSADORS CALLED "UP WITH PEOPLE," WHICH WAS MADE UP OF YOUNG ADULTS FROM EIGHTEEN DIFFERENT COUNTRIES. I HADN'T PLANNED ON THIS BUT, ON THE TOUR OF DACHAU, I ENDED UP WALKING JUST BEHIND TWO OF MY DEAR FRIENDS—ONE JEWISH, ONE GERMAN—AS THEY EXPERIENCED THE ENTIRE CAMP, LOCKED TOGETHER ARM-IN-ARM. I WAS VERY INTENTIONAL ABOUT STAYING CLOSE ENOUGH TO WITNESS THIS EXTREMELY POWERFUL MOMENT BETWEEN THEM, BUT I WAS FAR ENOUGH AWAY TO GIVE THEM THE SPACE THEY SEEMED TO DESIRE, AND TO NEED. THEY CRIED A LOT AS THEY WALKED THROUGH THE CAMP, AND SO DID I. MY FRIENDS WERE PART OF THE THEN-NEW GENERATION OF LEADERS

DETERMINED TO COME TOGETHER TO SHAPE A MUCH DIFFERENT WORLD, A WORLD WHERE GREAT CRIMES AGAINST HUMANITY, LIKE THE HOLOCAUST, WERE PART OF OUR HISTORY BUT WOULD HAVE NO PLACE IN OUR FUTURE.

★ ★

A tour of Dachau will shake you to your core. If you're unable to travel there right now, educate yourself about the Jewish Holocaust in other ways. Visit the United States Holocaust Memorial Museum in Washington, DC, or online at www.ushmm.org. Connect with someone who lived through it and allow them to enlighten you. Watch the moving documentary Paperclips. You can preview it at: www.youtube.com/watch?v=nEKIbzszoVo.

45

Way 23
Artistry in Motion

WITHOUT QUESTION, ONE OF THE MOST EXCELLENT DANCE AND THEATER COMPANIES IN THE WORLD IS THE ALVIN AILEY AMERICAN DANCE THEATER. CRITICALLY ACCLAIMED WORKS SUCH AS *REVELATIONS* AND *LOVE STORIES* ARE CONSIDERED SOME OF THE MOST BEAUTIFUL AND EXQUISITE EXPRESSIONS OF ART THROUGH DANCE THAT THE WORLD HAS EVER SEEN. I'VE BEEN FORTUNATE IN THAT I HAVE SEEN TWO OF THEIR COMPANIES PERFORM, ONE IN MICHIGAN AND THE OTHER IN NEW YORK CITY. DURING THE PERFORMANCES I JUST SAT IN MY SEAT LOOKING AS THOUGH MY JAW WAS UNHINGED AS I WATCHED THE DANCERS, COMPLETELY IN AWE AT THE VERY DEFINITION OF BEAUTY, BOLDNESS, AND PERFECTION BEFORE ME. AT TIMES, YOU COULD HEAR THE PEOPLE IN THE AUDIENCE GASP AT THE VISUAL POETRY ON THE STAGE.

A part of the AAADT experience that you might not expect is the audience itself, the eclectic crowd among which you will find yourself at any given performance. From blue jeans to tailor-made suits, cocktail dresses to camos, the Alvin Ailey audience is a beautiful mosaic. You can tell a lot about artists by the crowd that they draw. How diverse is the audience? Is their message universal enough to affect people who don't look like them? The art of Alvin Ailey is for everybody.

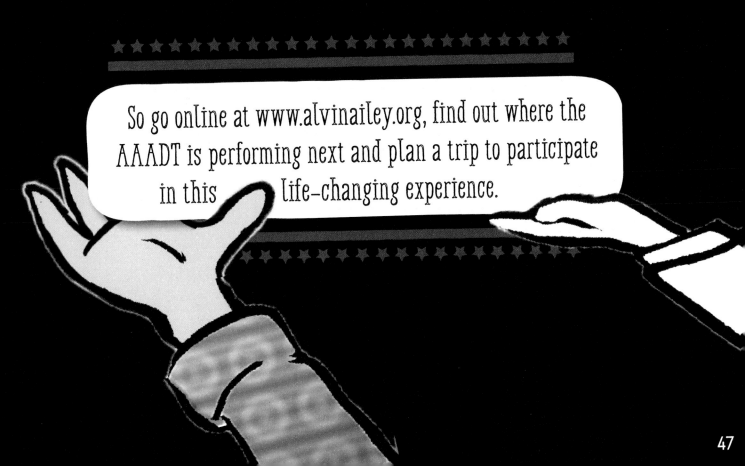

So go online at www.alvinailey.org, find out where the AAADT is performing next and plan a trip to participate in this life-changing experience.

"**A**T LEAST ONE OUT OF EVERY THREE WOMEN WORLDWIDE HAS BEEN THE VICTIM OF SEXUAL OR DOMESTIC VIOLENCE...OF THESE CRIMES, LESS THAN 50% ARE REPORTED TO THE POLICE."

This statement is from one of the most powerful books that I have ever read—*Half The Sky* by Nicholas D. Kristof and Sheryl WuDunn, which articulates, in often painful detail, some of the atrocities that women all over the world face. As a man, this was a wake-up call for me; I simply was unaware of some of the heartbreaking circumstances our sisters live with, the wrenching ordeals they are forced to endure, and how they are often blamed for their own victimization. There were times when I had to close the book because I couldn't take the violence. I was compelled, however, to open it back up as I thought about the fact that the women whose suffering I read about within those pages didn't have the option to simply turn the page or close the book.

Our sisters are no longer, however, enduring silently. And, I'm proud to say, they are no longer enduring alone as more and more men, like me, step up and speak up and stand with them. Here's a shout out to you, sistahs!

★★★★★★★★★★★★★★★★★★★★★★★★★★★★★

Become involved in the Half the Sky Movement, whose noble goal is to "turn oppression into opportunity for women worldwide." You can find them at *halftheskymovement.org*. Walk in a Take Back The Night rally, in support of ending sexual assault and domestic violence. Learn more at *takebackthenight.org*. Become a member of NOW—remember it is the National Organization *for* Women, not the National Organization *of* Women, and we men are welcomed as members with open arms! NOW is an iconic women's organization that has fought for women's rights for over fifty years now; visit them at *now.org*.

★★★★★★★★★★★★   ★★★★★★★★★

Way 25
A Heritage of Faith

PEOPLE OFTEN THINK OF THE CIVIL RIGHTS MOVEMENT AS BEING ONE THAT WAS FOR AFRICAN-AMERICANS ALONE. WHILE, YES, THE AFRICAN-AMERICAN COMMUNITY WAS A PRIMARY FOCUS OF THE MOVEMENT, THE CLEAR INTENT OF ITS LEADER, THE GREAT DR. MARTIN LUTHER KING, WAS TO FIGHT FOR THE RIGHTS OF ALL WHO WERE THE BRUNT OF SCORN, INJUSTICE AND VIOLENCE.

Some time ago I purchased a documentary that I consider a masterpiece—*Eyes on the Prize*. The film takes the viewer through a chronological journey of the movement that was a critically necessary force in not just African-American history, but all of American, indeed, world history. It was during this time that injustice was exposed for all the world to see, a sight that was necessary to change minds and hearts and light the path toward the most open society we are now free to experience and enjoy.

While we often think of leaders such as Medgar Evers, Martin Luther King, Fannie Lou Hamer, and Rosa Parks; one bit of enlightenment I took away from watching the documentary is that much of the forward progress of the movement was put in motion by teenagers, and their willingness to speak and act against Jim Crow segregation laws. Many of the innocent citizens who filled the jails back in the Civil Rights Era were middle grade and high school students. These young people of their time helped to shape a better, more just nation..

Watch *Eyes on the Prize*—you can purchase it here: www.shoppbs.org/product/index.jsp?productId=3999340. Make a trip with friends or family to the historic Civil Rights Museum in Memphis, Tennessee—or even simply visit them online at www.civilrightsmuseum.org—and you will quickly realize that freedom is, indeed, about one race— the human race. It's for you, it's for me; it's for all of us

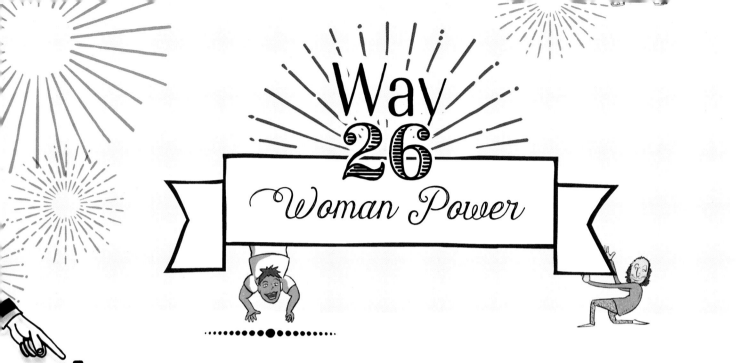

Way 26
Woman Power

LET'S GET REAL PRACTICAL ABOUT THIS: WITHOUT WOMEN, THERE WOULD BE NO ME TO WRITE THIS BOOK AND NO YOU TO READ IT. INDEED, IT WAS PROBABLY WOMEN, YOUR MOTHER AND YOUR GRANDMOTHER AND YOUR FIRST GRADE TEACHER—SEVENTY-SIX PERCENT OF U.S. GRADE SCHOOL TEACHERS ARE FEMALE (*NCES.ED.GOV/FASTFACTS/DISPLAY.ASP?ID=28*)— WHO TAUGHT YOU MOST OF THE FOUNDATIONAL SKILLS YOU POSSESS, INCLUDING HOW TO READ!

Yet, for centuries, women have been relegated to a subservient role in our societies—there was a time in history when women were not even allowed to vote and, unfortunately, in some countries that is still the case. Think about this, folks, it was only 1920 when the 19th Amendment to the United States Constitution was put into place that gave women in the U.S. the right to vote. That's less than a hundred years ago, not even half of the years the United States has been in existence!

I'm not saying that we haven't come a long way in recognizing the contributions women made and continue to make in our world, but I'm still bothered by the lack of parity. For example, the number of women in leadership positions in both for-profit and not-for-profit organizations doesn't come anywhere near the number of men who hold positions of power. Or, what about the inequality in pay between a man and a woman with the same qualifications? But remember that women make up over half of our world's population, and organizations that don't have the critical voice of women at the table are organizations that risk being irrelevant.

I believe that one of the best ways to stay relevant is to have a firm grasp of the context of your own relevancy. And there's no better way to do that than by having a working knowledge of history. Read *America's Women: 400 Years of Dolls, Drudges, Helpmates, and Heroines* by Gail Collins and you'll gain a deeper understanding of what it has been like to be a woman through the centuries on these shores.

Way 27
Who Am I?

I BELIEVE THAT OVER THE HEADS OF MOST EVERY PERSON ON THE PLANET HANGS AN INVISIBLE QUESTION MARK. THE QUESTION IS: WHO AM I? WHY AM I HERE? FROM WHENCE DID I COME? HOW DID I GET TO BE WHO I AM?

Identity—or, I should more clearly say, lack of identity—is, in my opinion, one of the single most global issues of our time. A person's sense of identity is what helps her or him feel as if they belong instead of merely being welcomed. A person's sense of identity is what gives him or her the foundation from which to make good decisions about their lives. Identity gives us a firm understanding of who we are, and that provides us with the ability to treat others in ways that are just and humane.

There is an old saying: If you don't stand for something, you will fall for anything. This is so very true because the person who has no idea who he or she is can be manipulated and tricked into being whoever someone else—a controlling spouse, an abusive boss, a cruel dictator—tells him or her she is.

Identity—that profoundly comfortable place of knowing yourself at your very core—is a much deeper issue than simply knowing which country or continent from which your people emigrated. A working knowledge of your own genealogy, however, is surely a great place to start. I remember watching a documentary on PBS, *African American Lives: Finding Your Roots*, by Dr. Henry Louis Gates, in which he traced the genetic legacy of a star-studded cast that included, among others, Sir Richard Branson, Keenen Ivory Wayans, Senator John McCain and Shonda Rhimes. I watched in wonder at how each of them reacted when he revealed what their genes told about their ancestral story. It was powerful to see how deeply touched these individuals were by the revelations, as if they could now place themselves like pins on a map—they were now "located."

Research your ancestry and find out about the great people from which you have come. Here's one resource to help you begin your journey: www.familytreedna.com.

Way 28
Hoopin' it Up

ON APRIL 24, 1996, SPORTS WENT TO THE NEXT LEVEL—THAT'S THE DAY THE WOMEN'S NATIONAL BASKETBALL ASSOCIATION WAS BORN. SHERYL SWOOPES, A THREE-TIME OLYMPIC GOLD MEDAL WINNER, WAS THE FIRST PLAYER SIGNED TO THE NEW LEAGUE AND NOW, JUST A COUPLE OF DECADES LATER, THE WNBA HAS BECOME A FIXTURE IN MODERN-DAY SPORTS CULTURE.

Even so, too many guys still think they should have the only say in sports—which sports are legitimate, which aren't; who should be allowed to play, and who shouldn't. The women of the WNBA, who serve as remarkable examples of the grace, tenacity, and amazing skill of women athletes, are changing that attitude one tip-off, one foul shot at a time.

This is critical for the young women coming up after them, so that those youngsters can see how broad and far they themselves might dream. The WNBA is a leader when it comes to inspiring our girls, chipping away at the glass ceiling with real swagger, towards the day when it is ultimately shattered for good.

Go to a WNBA game and cheer for your favorite team. Here's their website: http://www.wnba.com.

Way 29
Switcheroo

"SALES DOESN'T GET IT."

"Finance is always so tight with the resources."

"Why can't marketing understand our sense of urgency?"

It's easy to throw stones at other departments, and even other professions, until you actually have to do their job. Now, I know that that is not the normal reason for job swapping, which is generally done for a proper transition, or for professional development of some sort. Sometimes, however, it would just be a good thing to do it to foster a greater sense of humility and organizational understanding amongst peers.

It is going to be less difficult to understand why some facet of your organization isn't working the way you think it should after you've seen how the job is done from the inside. Or, maybe you've been thinking about changing jobs? You've thought about what it might be like to be a visual artist, work in finance, run a happenin' restaurant—and maybe, like after you've had to wait twenty minutes for table service, you've even thought you could do the job better than the people who were serving you. Well, why don't you talk to someone who currently does a job you don't understand, or that you think you'd like to do, and ask to shadow them for a day? I'm not saying you could or should make any major decisions on their behalf, but you would get a feel for what their job is all about.

Many people wait to experiment or test different waters after they retire, or after they've had some great epiphany. My question is: What the heck are you waiting for? Job swap or job shadow with someone else for a day.

Way 30
Eating, Fat and Lean

In our society, we have a media that presents impossibly perfect, more-frequently-than-not photo-shopped ideals of physical appearance, and too many of us accept them as attainable. We "fat shame" people who don't or can't live up to these unworkable ideals; or, at the other end, the quest to achieve the ideal drives people to dangerous relationships with their bodies. According to estimates from the National Institute of Mental Health, between five and ten per cent of girls and women—that is, five to ten million people—and one million boys and men suffer from eating disorders, including anorexia, bulimia, binge eating disorder, or other associated dietary conditions. If we take the time to understand the people who live without a good relationship to their bodies, who have poor

OR DISTORTED BODY IMAGES, WE MIGHT SEE THE EFFORT TO ACHIEVE A HEALTHY WEIGHT FOR WHAT IT IS: A DAY-TO-DAY STRUGGLE TO MAKE THE RIGHT EATING CHOICES, TO BREAK OUT OF A VICIOUS CYCLE OF BEING DEPRESSED BECAUSE THEY DIDN'T EAT RIGHT, AND THEN NOT EATING RIGHT BECAUSE THEY ARE DEPRESSED. USING THEIR RELATIONSHIP TO FOOD AS A SUBSTITUTE FOR THEIR RELATIONSHIPS WITH SELF-ESTEEM AND, OFTEN, FOR THE APPROVAL OF OTHERS.

As a society, we need to reframe our concepts of beauty from standards that are impossible to reach because they are wildly unrealistic, and start embracing how beautiful good health looks on everyone. Perhaps you or someone you know suffers from an eating disorder? If you want to help them with their struggle, you need to have a better understanding of exactly what that struggle is all about. Learn about eating disorders. Here's a great source to get you started: www.anad.org.

Way 31
The Isms

THE ATMOSPHERE IN THE ROOM WAS TENSE. AT TIMES TEARS FLOWED, AND SOMETIMES VOICES WERE RAISED. IT WAS, HOWEVER, A TRANSFORMATIVE MOMENT FOR EVERYONE IN THE ROOM, INCLUDING ME.

My initial reaction to attending an Institute for Healing Racism workshop was, Why do I need to do this? As a person of color I had a very deep and personal understanding of racism. But then I thought, I really don't know how white people experience racism. What they think about it. If we are going to overcome racism, don't both sides need to have a clearer understanding of each other's perceptions?

In a world that is, every day, becoming more global and multicultural, it just doesn't make sense for anyone to walk around oblivious of how our fellow human beings experience their own reality, their own ability to live happily and

productively in the social and cultural environment we share. L[a]
[aware]ness of how others are able to move through the world limits our
leaders, teachers, even friends.
[Wh]ile I can well understand why people will try to avoid confronting t[his]
[rac]ism—it's a hard conversation, and we don't yet have the vocabula[ry]
[al]low us to accept such a challenge with both gravity and sensitivit[y]
to stop being in denial about this most obvious elephant in the [room]
[facing] our fears is the only way we will be able to overcome them, an[d]
affect our world, and the world we are creating for future generat[ions]

★ ★

The Institute for Healing Racism workshop was a sobering, no-holds-barred encounter. Stop avoiding the hard conversation. Embrace the challenge. Participate in an Institute for Healing Racism workshop. IHR workshops are organized locally; here's a link to get you started on organizing one in your area: www.grcc.edu/thebobandaleiciawoodrickcenterforequityandinclusion/programs/instituteforhealingracism0. You might also want to read one of Nathan Rutstein's wonderful books, such as *Healing Racism in America*.

Way 32
Surf's Up

JUST ONE QUICK INTERNET SEARCH OF THE WORD DIVERSITY AND YOU'LL SEE THAT IT'S A TOPIC OF DISCUSSION ALL AROUND THE WORLD. IF YOU THINK ABOUT IT, IT MAKES SENSE—IT DOESN'T MATTER WHAT ORGANIZATION, WHAT COMMUNITY, OR WHAT COUNTRY YOU'RE TALKING ABOUT, YOU'LL FIND PEOPLE OF DIFFERENT BACKGROUNDS AND BELIEFS WHO'VE COME TOGETHER TO MAKE A WHOLE. AND THAT'S ONLY GOING TO BECOME EVER MORE THE CASE AS THE WORLD AND ITS MARKETS BECOME EVER MORE GLOBAL.

I have, particularly in the West, encountered the mindset that diversity is primarily a function of people looking different from each other. But shake off the Western mindset and think of diversity simply as differences. You are African-American and your friend is Euro-American.

You are Christian and your friend is an atheist. You are politically liberal and your friend is politically conservative. How many of those things can you tell about us just by looking at these two people? You can see my point.

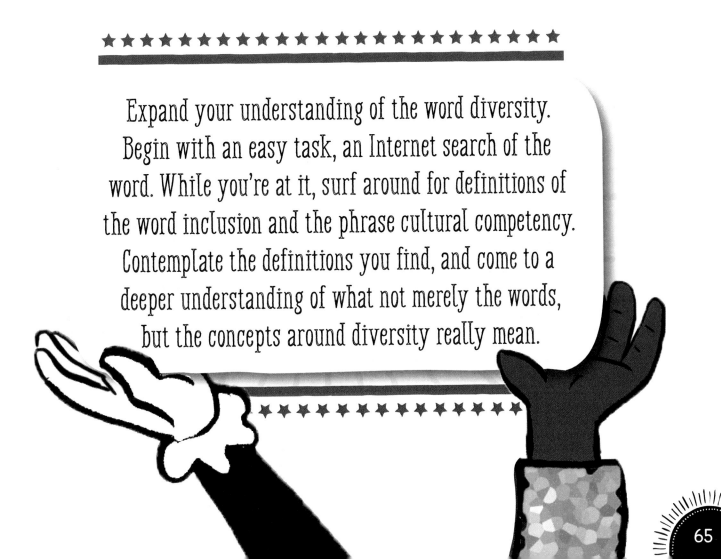

Expand your understanding of the word diversity. Begin with an easy task, an Internet search of the word. While you're at it, surf around for definitions of the word inclusion and the phrase cultural competency. Contemplate the definitions you find, and come to a deeper understanding of what not merely the words, but the concepts around diversity really mean.

Way 33

Viva La TV

MY WIFE, BARBARA, AND I HAVE COMMITTED TO LEARN SPANISH. IT'S A BEAUTIFUL LANGUAGE, AND SPANISH SPEAKERS ARE AN IMPORTANT PART OF THE FABRIC OF THE "NEW AMERICA."

One of the things that Barbara does to help her learn is to watch shows on a television network whose programming is in Spanish. That's both a practical and powerful way to hone your language skills. You begin to develop a better understanding of the cadence or rhythm of the language, and your novice attempts at conversation quickly begin to sound much more as if you're a native speaker.

Learning a new language, especially one that we in the U.S. could actually use on a daily basis, is simply practical. But learning any new language opens up doors of opportunity for new friendships and business relationships that might not have worked without your growing language skill.

When Barbara and I took our most recent trip to Mexico, we were able to order our food in Spanish, and greet the people we met along our daily strolls in their own language. Our efforts let them know that their culture, and their country, and they themselves, mattered to us, and the smiles we received in return were such a huge reward for what is, really, a small effort.

Immersion in a culture is an efficient way to learn a language. If you can't spend six months in Mexico learning Spanish, or a year in China learning Mandarin, make time to watch networks that offer programming in the language you're trying to learn. If, like us, you're trying to learn Spanish, Univision is a good place to begin—check them out at: www.univision.com.

Way 34
Seeing is Feeling

ONE OF THE LANGUAGES THAT IS OFTEN OVERLOOKED WHEN WE SPEAK OF LANGUAGE SKILLS IS BRAILLE, THE LANGUAGE USED BY THE VISUALLY IMPAIRED LIKE JOSE FELICIANO, HELEN KELLER, AND RAY CHARLES. JUST THIS SHORT ROSTER SHOWS US THAT THOUGH SOMEONE'S SIGHT MAY BE NON-EXISTENT, HIS OR HER VISION CAN BE VAST. WHO WOULD ARGUE THAT STEVIE WONDER IS NOT ONE OF THE GREATEST VISIONARY MUSICIANS IN MODERN HISTORY? YET, HE HAS BEEN WITHOUT SIGHT FOR MOST OF HIS LIFE.

The ingenuity that it took for Louis Braille, who was blind himself, to create a language for those without sight rather stuns me every time I think about it. It is an amazing invention that has equipped countless generations to communicate and connect. We think of our fingertips as sensitive, but the sensitivity to actually read with them? That's a real skill.

To gain an appreciation for those who read with their fingertips, I've got a travel challenge for you—and that's because hotels are pretty darned good at making their guest rooms Braille-friendly. Learn to feel numbers and distinguish them. Then, next time you're at a hotel, take the elevator to your floor and close your eyes—and try to find your room by feeling the room numbers on the doorways outside the rooms. Those of us who are not fluent in Braille, however, should be sure to have a friend with us whose eyes are wide open—like speaking any other language, reading Braille isn't generally something one can pick up overnight, and for those of us who are accustomed to seeing everything with our eyes, there is the possibility of falling, tripping, and bumping into walls as we learn to navigate that hotel hallway without sight.

Way 35

One Family

ALL HUMAN BEINGS SHARE ABOUT 98% OF OUR BIOLOGICAL MAKEUP—THAT IS, 98% OF OUR GENES ARE IDENTICAL TO EVERY OTHER HUMAN BEING ON THE FACE OF THE EARTH. THE GENETIC DIFFERENCES AMONG US ARE QUITE SMALL—THE AMOUNT OF MELANIN IN OUR SKIN, OUR HAIR COLOR, AND OUR EYE COLOR—WHICH IS WHAT THE REMAINING 2% OF OUR GENES DETERMINE.

Unfortunately, judging from the way we sometimes treat each other, you might think that each different color came from a different planet. The blame for that lies with a man by the name of Johann Friedrich Blumenbach (1752-1840), a German naturalist who developed and codified one of the earliest human racial classification systems. It was he who positioned those whose ancestors were perceived to come from the

Caucasus mountains as the top "race" and those whose ancestors were perceived to come from the continent of Africa as the bottom one. Once the culture bought into his lie, it was easy for the top "race" to justify the mistreatment of those who were not on the top of the hierarchy. His pseudoscience—Eugenics—is what helped to justify the cultural toxicity of slavery, and ultimately became the foundation for Jim Crow segregation, and the continued racism we have to deal with today. The word race still means something in the mainstream culture. It shouldn't.

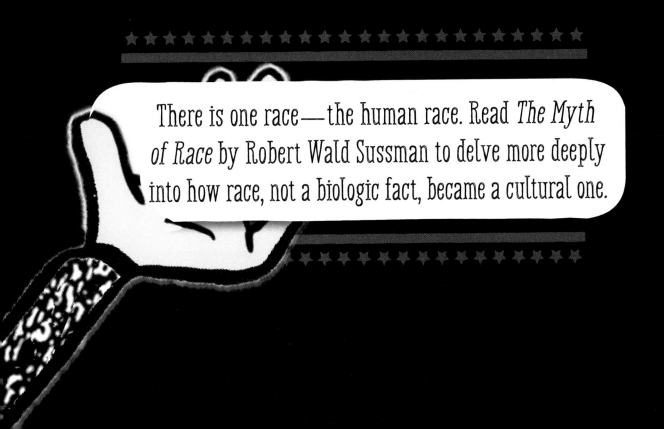

There is one race—the human race. Read *The Myth of Race* by Robert Wald Sussman to delve more deeply into how race, not a biologic fact, became a cultural one.

Way 36
So Much in Common

ONE THING I KNOW FOR SURE IS THAT DREAMS FOR A BETTER LIFE ARE NOT A GEOGRAPHICAL PHENOMENON. YOU CAN SEE INTENT IN THE EYES OF THE CHILD IN GRAND RAPIDS AND IN THE EYES OF THE ELDER IN THE VILLAGE IN GHANA. THAT'S BECAUSE, AT OUR CORE, WE HUMAN BEINGS ARE MORE ALIKE THAN WE ARE DIFFERENT.

Many years ago, a friend and I passed a young person of color *peeing on the sidewalk*. We were both aghast at his actions, but my friend, who was white, said to me, "Man, your people need to do better!"

Your people? I was taken aback that it might *not* have occurred to him that white people have also done things as uncouth and unpleasant as peeing on a street, but, what I really wanted him to do was to consider his statement on a deeper level. To understand that the only thing distinguishing my people from his people was the color of our skins.

At the end of the day, every person on Earth cries, hurts, celebrates, gets tired, laughs. We cannot dismiss each other with the idea of "your people" if we want to live in an "us" reality.

★ ★

Spend your lunch hour people watching. Sit on a park bench or nip into a busy museum. Focus on the individuals who might normally make up only the background of your vision, and your consciousness—the elderly couple, the reluctant child, the museum guard. Let yourself consider that this person has dreams and goals as important to them as yours are to you—you know really nothing about the guard but, if you sat together over a coffee at the museum café, he could tell you a story that would amaze you.

Way 37
There's Only One You

IF TWO OF US ARE EXACTLY IDENTICAL, THEN ONE OF US IS UNNECESSARY. YOU ARE THE YOU-EST YOU THERE IS, NO ONE CAN BEAT YOU AT IT—YOU ARE FEARFULLY AND WONDERFULLY MADE.

Unfortunately, most everything in our culture urges us to blend in, to fit it, to keep our heads down so we don't stand out. Take the example of mainstream fashion—fashion editors saturate their pages with the "trends" of the season, and retailers fill their stores with the prescribed "look", and then we are allowed the privilege of buying outfits that are manufactured by the thousands so we can all look alike—at least for this one season, until the fashion designers and editors and retailers tell us it's time for all of us to switch it up again.

I live in Michigan, where we have all four seasons, so I know a few things

snow. One thing I know about it is that of all the billions of snow
have ever fallen from the sky, not one of them is identical to any othe
ct that every school child knows, and embraces with wonder. In
t could be like if we embraced with the same wonder the idea that
billion individuals now living on planet Earth, not one is identical

★ ★

One of my favorite thinkers, Seth Godin, said in his book, *Linchpin*, "You can either stand out or fit in, but you can't do both." Take a few minutes before you go to sleep to reflect on your day. Think of what you did, and how you acted and reacted, what made you laugh, what annoyed you, what motivated you, what did you dismiss as trivial or, at least, not a priority. Realize that no one else on Earth—not one among your seven billion fellow human beings—would have done it exactly as you have. Let yourself absolutely love how unique you are.

Way 38
Motivational Listener

IN MY UNDERGRAD DAYS, I WAS A COMMUNICATIONS AND BROADCAST-ING MAJOR, WHICH MEANT THAT I HAD TO TAKE OVER THIRTY CLASSES IN MY MAJOR. OUT OF ALL OF THOSE CLASSES *NOT ONE OF THEM FOCUSED ON LISTENING.* THIS WASN'T A DISPARITY THAT STRUCK ME AT THE TIME; IT IS ONLY AS I'VE GROWN AND SPENT TIME OUT IN THE REAL, BUSINESS-ORIENTED WORLD, THAT I UNDERSTAND WHAT A REAL DEFICIT THIS WAS.

I've had lots of people hand me business cards that list "motivational speaker" as their job title, but not one person has ever handed me a card that said "motivational listener."

In our global culture, the emphasis is too often on what you say and not what you know. But show me a politician who listens to her or his constituents and I'll show you a great leader. Show me a father who listens to his family and I'll show you happy kids. Show me a husband and wife who listen to each other and I'll show you a strong marriage.

Listening is a discipline that isn't innate; it takes energy, focus and time—all the things that our fast-paced society doesn't afford you unless you are intentional about it.

In my consulting work, I spend a lot of time listening. It's listening that helps me to ask better questions of my clients, as well as to discern areas of concern that they may not bring up directly, either because they don't have the vocabulary to do so, or because they themselves don't yet know they've got a specific difficulty that needs to be addressed, or compromise that needs to be reached.

Sound expert Julian Treasure has some brilliant advice for those of us who aspire to hone our listening skills. Check out his TED talk at www.ted.com/talks/julian_treasure_5_ways_to_listen_better.

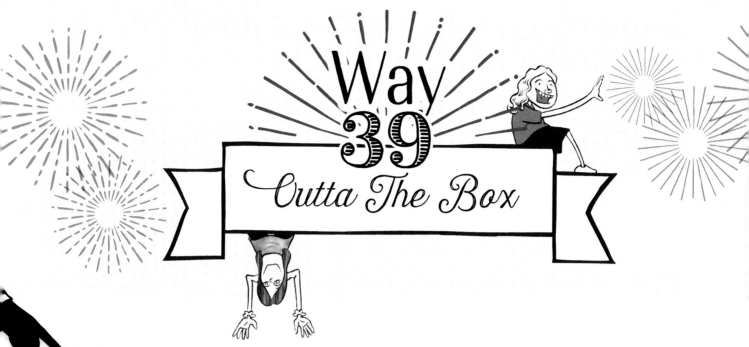

Way 39

Outta The Box

"THINK OUTSIDE OF THE BOX." HOW MANY TIMES HAVE WE HEARD THIS PHRASE? PROBABLY FAR TOO MANY, BUT IT'S STILL A WAY WE ALL NEED TO THINK.

A few years ago, I was preparing to speak at a conference of women global leaders and the topic they had asked me to speak about was how to think outside of the box. I immediately began to think about how I could say something different about this apt but overused phrase—how I could do something out of the box with it—and, while I was pondering, it occurred to me that there was a part of the phrase that we all accepted but no one, to my knowledge, had addressed head on: The simple fact that there is a box.

There are two parts to a box, the lid and the box itself, that can both serve as

...hors for containment. First, the box itself is a metaphor for hori...

...sion, or how people tend to minimize their own ability to expan...

...reas, begin new adventures, take on new risks. The other part of...

...l, which is a metaphor for vertical limits, or how the expectation...

...nce of others usurp or prevent our upward ascension to the nex...

...life. Some people might try to "keep the lid on us" because they f...

...fety and security if we step too far out into the world; and others n...

...f down the lid on our box because they're threatened by how mu...

...achieve if we have the freedom to bring a big dream to fruition. In...

...he lid that's clamped down on our box is the same one.

★★★★★★★★★★★★★★★★★★★★★★★★★★★★★★★★

There is a provocative question that I just love: What would you do if you knew you could not fail? Spend an evening contemplating that question. Write down your answers on a sheet of paper. Allow yourself to focus on your dreams, and what you might accomplish if the limits you place on yourself—or the limits society places on you, particularly those placed on you by other folks—were shattered.

Way 40
Bridgebuilder

I LOVE THE TERM "BRIDGE BUILDER" SO MUCH THAT I NAMED MY CONSULTING FIRM AFTER IT—GLOBAL BRIDGEBUILDERS. THE TERM SPEAKS TO THE FUNCTION OF A BRIDGE, A STRUCTURE THAT ALLOWS US TO CROSS FROM ONE PLACE TO ANOTHER, OFTEN OVER A CHASM THAT WOULD BE IMPASSABLE WITHOUT SUCH A PIECE OF INFRASTRUCTURE.

The integrity of any bridge determines the amount of weight it can bear. Some bridges can bear only the weight of bicycles; others are engineered to handle large amounts of heavy traffic. For example, in the 1950s, people in the Euro-American culture began, however tentatively, to cross the African-American bridge to listen to what was then termed "race music"—and, as the generations since can attest, what was once a footbridge is now the rock 'n' roll super highway.

As we walk back and forth across these sorts of bridges, we take part of the experience of a new culture with us. In doing so, "cultural exchange" occurs. The culture we've visited changes and is enriched, and so is our own.

Every bridge that has ever been built began as the dream of a single person. One person sees the need or the possibility, and then enlists others in his or her vision. We reach out to one fellow human being to create a connection and, with each new connection, our bridge becomes stronger, takes us farther, grows more beautiful.

★ ★

Build your own bridge, or make the one you're already constructing more sturdy. Walk next door and welcome your new neighbor to the neighborhood. Volunteer to work the snack stand at your local Little League games. Visit for a few minutes with the shopkeeper instead of only making your purchase and moving right on with your busy day. Connect.

★ ★ ★ ★ ★ ★ ★   ★ ★ ★ ★ ★ ★ ★ ★ ★

Way 41
Tolerating Tolerance

HUMAN BEINGS WERE DESIGNED TO BE LIFE-LONG LEARNERS. AS SUCH, WE SHOULD ALWAYS HAVE OUR INTELLECTUAL RADAR ON, READY TO QUESTION, AND EVEN TO CHALLENGE, THE TERMS UNDER WHICH SOCIETY ASKS US TO ENGAGE. TOLERANCE IS ONE SUCH TERM THAT NEEDS TO BE CHALLENGED.

Hang nails, traffic jams, a delay on the tarmac—these are things we don't like but which we tolerate because there's pretty much no way of getting through modern life without experiencing them. But I get downright itchy when, in diversity discussions, well-meaning people use the words tolerate or tolerance in reference to people. Frankly, I can't understand why it's even a concept we still use when we talk about ways we can deal with or react to people who are different from ourselves.

Part of my job is giving talks, often in front of huge groups of people at a time. Whenever the "t" word comes up, I like to do an informal poll. "How many of you want to be tolerated?" I'll ask. My question is always met with stunned silence, and not one hand goes up. No one wants to be merely tolerated, as if the way they dress, or the church they attend, or the color of their skin is akin to a bad smell that makes someone want to cover his nose in order to endure. Indeed, it is not in the heart of any person, made in the image of God, to accept that they are being tolerated. People, all people, deserve more than meager tolerance.

Find something in your life that you tolerate—the resignation of a husband or wife to a spouse using his or her razor even though they've been asked for going on a decade not to do that, the refusal of the child who won't eat the carrot and celery sticks you pack in her lunch every day, that sticky screen door that never closes without a squeak no matter how you oil the hinge. Are any of these things, irritating as they might be on a day-to-day basis, in any way comparable to a fellow human being? Go beyond tolerance. Move on to truly value and celebrate.

Way 42
Put It In Black and White

RICK WILSON, MY "BROTHER FROM ANOTHER MOTHER," PASSED AWAY RECENTLY. HE AND I HOSTED A WEEKLY RADIO SHOW TOGETHER CALLED *RADIO IN BLACK AND WHITE*—WHAT WE RIGHTLY DUBBED "THE MOST INTEGRATED HOUR OF THE WEEK"—AND I DON'T THINK I'LL EVER STOP MISSING THE CONVERSATIONS HE AND I HAD IN THAT BRIEF HOUR EVERY WEEK. THE PURPOSE OF OUR SHOW WAS TO DEMYSTIFY THIS THING CALLED CULTURE AND DEBUNK STEREOTYPES IN ORDER TO BEGIN TO BUILD TRUE COMMUNITY WITH ONE ANOTHER, THROUGH REAL, SOMETIMES DIFFICULT BUT ALWAYS NECESSARY, CONVERSATION.

I am not, in general, any kind of fan of PC dialogue or politically correct anything. Right here and now, let me distinguish overtly insulting or offensive comments from what I regard as PC: refraining from being proactively offensive in conversation is merely being a decent and humane human being, but refraining from productive discussion because the people having the conversation are too timid to ask provocative questions or express challenging opinions—well, that makes for some boring exchanges, doesn't it? Rick disliked the beating-around-the-bush sort of PC dialogue as much as I do, so there was rarely a dull moment on our show. We interviewed everyone from white supremacists to folks who wanted to organize a professional all-white basketball league—that is, folks who were, often diametrically, in opposition to the worldview that we shared.

We did this in the interest of creating a more multi-ethnic brother- and sisterhood of the sort that Rick and I shared. Please don't live your life without listening to, and loving, people who aren't just like you. You will surely miss out on the richness that life truly has to offer.

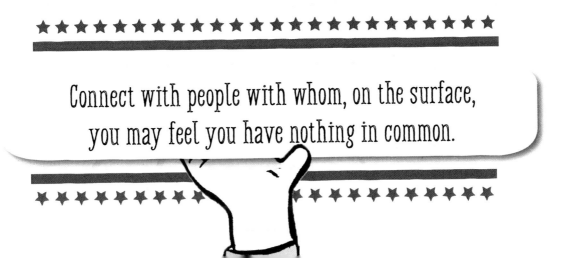

Connect with people with whom, on the surface, you may feel you have nothing in common.

Way 43
A Ministry of Presence

VIBRANT HEALTH IS TRULY A PRECIOUS GIFT—AND ONE NOT EVERYONE ENJOYS OR, FOR THAT MATTER, NOT ONE THAT ANYBODY ENJOYS ALL THE TIME. THERE ARE MANY HURTING PEOPLE IN THE WORLD, AND SOME OF THEM FIND THEMSELVES UNDER THE CARE OF A HOSPITAL STAFF. LET ME SAY RIGHT HERE, BEFORE ANYONE CAN MISCONSTRUE MY INTENTION, THAT THE VAST MAJORITY OF FOLKS WHO WORK IN HOSPITALS DO SO BECAUSE THEY THEMSELVES HAVE A CALLING OR SPECIAL GIFTS—THE GIFTS OF HEALING AND COMPASSION. BUT I KNOW A LOT OF FOLKS WHO WORK IN HOSPITALS PERSONALLY AND NOT ONE OF THEM HAS EVER EVEN INTIMATED THAT THEY'VE GOT ENOUGH TIME ON THEIR SHIFT TO GIVE THE KIND OF PERSONAL CARE THAT A PATIENT'S FAMILY OR CLOSE FRIENDS CAN PROVIDE. SO, WHAT HAPPENS WHEN A HOSPITAL PATIENT DOESN'T HAVE THAT CIRCLE OF FAMILY AND FRIENDS TO STEP IN WHEN THEY NEED THEM? THIS IS WHERE YOU COME IN.

I call making the time to visit the sick the "ministry of presence." It doesn't require any special skill at all, only the basic human instincts that are the desire to comfort and to be of use. A smile. A gentle hand to hold. A song, if you're so inclined. A get-well card, or a bunch of flowers if you've got a few dollars to spare. The purpose of your visit is simply to send a message to someone who is suffering: You are not forgotten.

The added benefit is that it is quite possible you will walk away from that sick room encouraged and uplifted yourself. Because that's just how love works—when you give it away, it multiplies.

An encouraging presence has more power than any of us can imagine—until we are in need of it ourselves. Visit someone who's stuck in the hospital—you may just make their day, as well as your own.

Way 44
Be a Local

BIG BOX STORES SURE DO MAKE IT EASY, AND OFTEN CHEAP, TO SHOP.

I'd like to suggest, however, that in the search for a convenient bargain, you don't overlook local innovators. From neighborhood restaurants to art galleries featuring hometown talent to the auto repair where the mechanic knows not only your name but also the quirks of your particular car, there are some incredibly creative and industrious people making a go of it in every town and city in this country.

If a community is to truly be vibrant and strong, much of its strength must come from its local people *because they live there.* They are the ones involved in the PTA, the neighborhood associations, the local service organizations. They specifically aren't the big box stores who choose their locations only for the revenue they can generate for the bottom line; locals are in any given community because it is home and they have a stake in making it a great place to live.

While you're in the process of shopping local, make sure to go outside of your immediate neighborhood to support the businesses of people who don't look like you, or may not even speak the same language you do. A friend of mine decided to stop at the Mexican food truck she'd passed for years, at which she'd only ever seen Mexican day laborers gathered to purchase their lunches. She was rewarded with the best taquitos she'd ever tasted—and the food truck's owners got an infusion of new customers based on her glowing reviews. In order for a community to truly thrive, all parts of the local economy must thrive, and you can play a direct part in that.

Take yourself shopping for a day, and purchase only items from locally-owned, small businesses.

Way 45
Honor and Pride

I TRAVEL QUITE A BIT, WHICH MEANS I SPEND MORE THAN MY FAIR SHARE OF TIME IN AIRPORTS, AND I AM ALWAYS IN ADMIRATION OF OUR FOLKS IN MILITARY UNIFORMS. WHETHER THEY ARE GOING HOME FOR A SURPRISE VISIT OR BEING DEPLOYED, I APPRECIATE THEM IMMENSELY; I ALWAYS GREET THEM WHEN THEY PASS WITH A QUICK BUT HEARTFELT, "THANK YOU FOR YOUR SERVICE," AND MY HEART SWELLS WHEN A LINE OF OUR UNIFORMED PERSONNEL MARCHES BY AND MY FELLOW TRAVELERS ARE MOVED TO APPLAUD AS THEY PASS. THEIR ALWAYS HUMBLE SMILES OF ACKNOWLEDGMENT AND GRATITUDE STAY WITH ME FOR A LONG TIME.

Although I am sure we share a mutual admiration for our service members, I'll bet you've never thought of them as a minority. Well, it's true—they are! Our country has sent military men and women on active

yment to foreign wars for well over a decade now, and still o
r population—one percent!—has a family member or even k
one who is on active duty.

citizens, supporting our military service men and women isr
thing we should do, whenever we might have the time or inclir
r duty to support those men and women who, whether we know
nally or not, are willing to make the ultimate sacrifice in order th
us remain free and at peace.

★ ★

Former First Lady Michelle Obama made it one of her missions while in office to enlarge the nation's support for our military service men and women, and their families as well. If you haven't yet extended her legacy of honoring our military by lending your home-front care, it's never too late to get involved. The American Red Cross is a good place to start looking for a way you can give back to those who give so much:

redcross.org/about-us/our-work
/military-families.

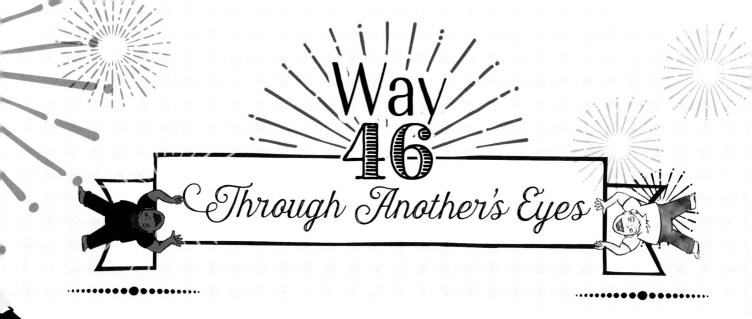

Way 46
Through Another's Eyes

DO YOU REMEMBER, A FEW PAGES AGO, I TOLD YOU ABOUT INTERVIEWING A WHITE SUPREMACIST FOR MY RADIO SHOW, *RADIO IN BLACK AND WHITE*? SINCE I AM AFRICAN-AMERICAN, YOU MIGHT THINK THAT I WOULD BE RELUCTANT TO HAVE A CONVERSATION WITH SUCH A PERSON. YOU'D BE WRONG. I WAS EAGER FOR THE CONVERSATION. I DIDN'T WANT TO UNTWIST HIS LOGIC, POINT OUT THE ERRORS IN HIS THINKING PROCESS, CHANGE HIS MIND... WELL, ALL RIGHT, YES, THERE IS ALWAYS THE HOPE OF BENEFITTING THE PERSON TO WHOM WE ARE SPEAKING, BUT AT MY CORE WHAT I WANTED FROM THIS GUEST WAS MUCH MORE FOR *MY* BENEFIT. I WANTED TO KNOW WHAT ABOUT HIS UPBRINGING, HIS EXPERIENCE, HIS EDUCATION HAD CAUSED HIM TO FORM AND ATTACH HIMSELF TO HIS BELIEFS. I WANTED TO LEARN FROM HIM.

Approaching my conversation with the white supremacist in this way completely disarmed him. It allowed him to open up to me, person-to-person, in a way he wouldn't have been able to if I'd rushed into the dialogue on the offensive. Indeed, at the end of the interview, the white supremacist confessed that he was used to people "attacking" him for his views; he was not used to people—especially people of color—listening to him with interest and compassion.

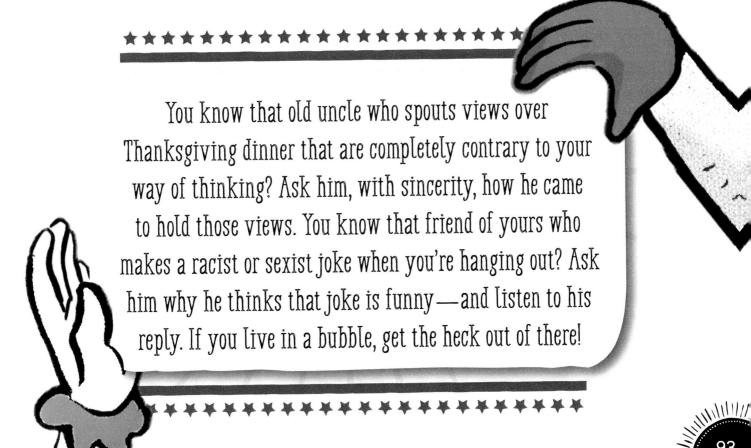

You know that old uncle who spouts views over Thanksgiving dinner that are completely contrary to your way of thinking? Ask him, with sincerity, how he came to hold those views. You know that friend of yours who makes a racist or sexist joke when you're hanging out? Ask him why he thinks that joke is funny—and listen to his reply. If you live in a bubble, get the heck out of there!

Way 47

Brother to Brother and Sister to Sister

I LOVE WATCHING THE SUMMER OLYMPICS AND, MORE SPECIFICALLY, THE RELAY RACES. THEY SEEM TO ME TO BE A METAPHOR FOR MANY THINGS ABOUT LIFE AND LEADERSHIP. THINK ABOUT IT: ONE OF THE MOST CRITICAL COMPONENTS OF THE RACE IS THE HAND-OFF. AN ATHLETE CAN RUN AND GIVE HIS OR HER TEAM AN AMAZING LEAD ONLY TO DROP THE BATON IN THE HAND-OFF. THIS CRITICAL MOMENT IS WHAT CAN TURN A GOLD-MEDAL PERFORMANCE INTO NO MEDAL AT ALL.

It is much the same in life: we must pass the baton to the next generation in a way that ensures they have all they need to be successful. Our success is ultimately measured by the up-and-coming generation—if we haven't left them a solid foundation, we have fumbled the hand-off... we have failed.

While there are many great organizations that help in the passing of the baton, one such long-standing initiative is Big Brothers Big Sisters, an organization that makes it easy and rewarding for you to invest your time to make sure that the next generation has what it needs to thrive. As Sir Isaac Newton said, "If I have seen farther than others, it is because I have stood on the shoulders of giants." No one is self-made; all of us need a helping hand from time to time. Be a giant to a young person in need of your hand-up.

Invest in the future of the next generation—
become a Big Brother or Big Sister.
Go here www.bbbs.org to get started.

Way 48
World Rhythms

TO MY FAMILY, TRAVEL IS A PRIORITY EXPENSE: SPENDING TIME AMONG PEOPLE OF VARIOUS CULTURES, EATING AND DANCING AND GOING TO CONCERTS AND MUSEUMS AND JUST, GENERALLY, *LEARNING*. AS I'VE ALREADY SAID, THERE ARE THREE MAIN WAYS PEOPLE EXPRESS THEIR CULTURES—VISUAL ARTS, FOOD, AND MUSIC; MY FAMILY AND I ARE ENTHUSIASTIC CONSUMERS, IF NOT ALWAYS CONNOISSEURS, OF EACH ONE OF THOSE WAYS. JUST HOW FAR AWAY I WAS FROM BEING AN EXPERT IN WORLD MUSIC WAS BROUGHT HOME TO ME BY MY DEAR COUSIN, THE ACCOMPLISHED SCHOLAR STERLING STUCKEY.

I am an avid music lover, with a particular bent toward Brazilian artists—even if I don't yet have full command of the Portuguese language and don't always understand all the lyrics. I found that I was intuiting so much about the culture from how the music was structured melodically; its syncopation seemed to me, in some vague but inescapable way, to encapsulate the history and traditions of the country. Sterling was the first person to describe my approach to music in scholarly terms.

"Ethnomusicology," he said—the study of music in its cultural context, including the country's history, folklore, linguistics, and psychology.

I was floored! The idea of studying a culture by way of its music was an absolutely delicious idea to me!

Musicology is a traditional area of study focusing on the history and literature of Western art music. Ethnomusicology is the study of all kinds of music as a social and cultural force within different countries, and even regions of countries. Institutions of higher learning in several countries as well as the U.S. offer courses in it. Locate one near you and become a student for a semester. Here's a comprehensive list of where ethnomusicology courses are offered: *http://www.ethnomusicology.org/?page=GtP.*

Way 49
A Great and Mighty Walk

DID YOU KNOW THAT PRIOR TO 1869 THERE WAS NO MIDDLE EAST? AT LEAST, NOT IN THE WAY WE KNOW IT TODAY. THE CONSTRUCTION OF THE SUEZ CANAL "CREATED" THE MIDDLE EAST. PRIOR TO THAT, IT WAS ALL CONSIDERED AFRICA.

Did you know that the very first university anywhere was in Timbuktu, in Mali, West Africa?

Did you know that Jesus wasn't a blonde-haired, blue-eyed European? Think about where the events in the Bible took place and you'll understand how impossible that concept of Jesus really is!

I am not a historian, but for many years I have had a very strong appetite to "unlearn" the incorrect history that I was taught through biased school books, the teachers who used them, and the media messages that were all around

. I soaked up books like *Lies My Teacher Told Me* by Dr. James W. L[...]
d Howard Zinn's *A People's History of the United States* in my quest [...]
tory right.

nd then a friend of mine, Stan Young, introduced me to one of the [...]
werful master teachers I have ever encountered—Dr. John Henrik C[...]
s documentary, *A Great and Mighty Walk*, is simply one of the [...]
standing history lessons I believe I've ever had. Watching it filled in [...]
he great gaps I had in my own understanding of history, and it is pres[...]
such a substantive yet accessible way that the viewer feels as if he is [...]
he feet of an elder, at last hearing the great truths.

History is a clock that people use to tell their political and cultural ti[...]
," Dr. Clarke says in the film.

truly believe that viewing this documentary is essential in understa[...]
only what time it is, but who sets the clock in the first place.

★★★★★★★★★★★★★★★★★★★★★★★★★★★★★★★★★★

Check out *A Great and Mighty Walk* by Dr. John Henrik Clarke and learn about world history from a different perspective: *www.youtube.com/watch?v=njdQzyQnHeg.*

Way 50
Soup's On

PERSPECTIVE IS A POWERFUL TEACHER, BUT MANY PEOPLE TEND TO THINK THAT THE ONLY VIEWS WITH VALUE ARE THE ONES THAT HAVE A UNIVERSITY CREDENTIAL OR DOLLAR SIGN ATTACHED TO THEM. NOT TRUE. THE VALUE OF A PERSON CANNOT BE DISCERNED BY THEIR TITLE OR BANK ACCOUNT. IT MUST BE DISCOVERED THROUGH CONVERSATION AND WALKING ALONG SIDE OF THEM.

Some years ago I served on the board of a mission. The sole purpose of that mission, although we didn't get it right all of the time, was to make sure that the invisible and voiceless in our city were both seen and heard. Each month we would gather in fellowship and hear from some of our clients. Those gatherings had a huge personal impact on me. Well-traveled as I am, it came as a surprise to me to find out at some of those earliest gatherings that some of the people we served in our mission had Masters' degrees, even a few PhDs. I grew very quiet as they told us their painful stories of how they ended up living in a shelter, eating in a soup kitchen.

One of the most powerful lessons I learned was that these homeless men and women were no less intelligent than any of us—most of them, through a series of events, had simply made wrong choices. Their wisdom is hard-won… and worth your attention.

★★★★★★★★★★★★★★★★★★★★★★★★★★★

Soup kitchens provide an unparalleled opportunity to meet a variety of people who are in between blessings but no less capable of teaching you, if you have ears to hear. Volunteer at a soup kitchen and make it your classroom. If you are a leader of a corporate team, create an opportunity for your management team to serve at a soup kitchen. But don't just serve the soup. Sit down and talk to the people while they eat. I guarantee the experience will be a rich one for all involved.

Way 51
Amandla

I F I WERE EVER TO LIVE IN ANOTHER REGION OF THE WORLD, IT WOULD BE IN SOUTHERN AFRICA—SHOUT OUT TO NAMIBIA! I'VE HAD THE OPPORTUNITY TO VISIT THE APARTHEID MUSEUM IN JOHANNESBURG, SOUTH AFRICA MANY TIMES, AND EACH TIME I GO THERE THE EXPERIENCE IS DIFFERENT FOR ME. I HAVE SPENT COUNTLESS HOURS WALKING FROM DISPLAY AREA TO DISPLAY AREA, AND I STILL FEEL AS IF I HAVEN'T TAKEN IN EVERYTHING THE MUSEUM HAS TO OFFER. I'M GRATEFUL TO THE PEOPLE OF SOUTH AFRICA FOR PUTTING THEIR HEARTS AND SOULS INTO THIS MUSEUM, FOR TELLING THE TRUTH ABOUT A PAINFUL HISTORY, YET I KNOW THERE ARE THOUSANDS OF STORIES YET UNTOLD. PLACES LIKE THE APARTHEID MUSEUM, THE HECTOR PIETERSON MUSEUM, THE DISTRICT 6 MUSEUM GIVE US AT LEAST A STARTING POINT.

Even through the most exhaustive effort, however, I understand that it would be nearly impossible to reflect hundreds of years of history under one roof. So while I am left always wanting more, I am also always satisfied by the one overarching theme that continues to speak to me in all my visits to the various museums. That is the passion and the resilience of the people of South Africa. They were determined to see freedom realized, and though the treatment to which they were subjected was unfathomably brutal and inhumane, they persevered. And realize freedom they did. Even though he's no longer with us, the movement's pinnacle leader, Nelson Mandela—or Madiba, as he was affectionately known—still stands as a model of humility, strength, and resolve for all people, whether or not they are from South Africa.

The South Africa of today is vastly different from the South Africa of yesterday. Yes, there are still areas of abject poverty, but there is also a growing middle class with their eyes on a bright and strong future.

Amandla is a Zulu and Xhosa word meaning power. Find out a bit more about apartheid and its history in South Africa—and the meaning of power. Here's your gateway: www.apartheidmuseum.org/#.

Way 52
Do You Hear What I See?

SHHH...DID YOU HEAR THAT? MANY OF OUR FELLOW HUMAN BEINGS MAY ANSWER NO. WE TAKE SO MANY THINGS FOR GRANTED AND, FOR HEARING PEOPLE, OUR HEARING IS SIMPLY ONE OF THEM. IMAGINE BEING WITHOUT THIS GIFT—TURN ON YOUR TV AND TURN OFF THE VOLUME TO GET AN IDEA OF WHAT PEOPLE LIKE BEETHOVEN, OPEOLUWA SOTONWA, HELEN KELLER, ROB LOWE, HOLLY HUNTER, AND PAUL STANLEY OF THE ROCK GROUP KISS EXPERIENCED AND CONTINUE TO EXPERIENCE ON A DAY-TO-DAY BASIS.

For the deaf and the hard of hearing, the battle for civil rights includes the right to linguistic freedom—that means having the American Sign Language (ASL) recognized as a language in its own right. It was among the freedoms for which deaf people and other advocates began fighting as long ago as 1880, and which continues today even as we see more and more ASL interpreters translating at events from Broadway plays to political speeches. Today, deaf people are both more able to thoroughly enjoy the sorts of entertainment that we hearing folks take for granted and more likely to be immediately included as citizens in events such as our president's annual State of the Union address.

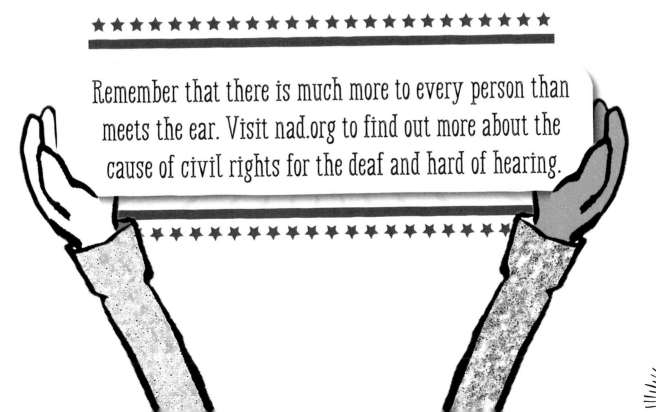

Remember that there is much more to every person than meets the ear. Visit nad.org to find out more about the cause of civil rights for the deaf and hard of hearing.

Way 53

Wisdom from Above

WE LIVE IN A WORLD SATURATED WITH INFORMATION—TECHNOLOGY HAS MADE FACTS AND STATISTICS AS AVAILABLE AS GOSSIP WAS IN THE DAYS BEFORE THE ABILITY TO INSTANTLY FACT-CHECK ON A SMART PHONE, THOUGH WHETHER A FACT IS "TRUE" OR NOT DEPENDS ENTIRELY ON THE WEB SITE ANY ONE INDIVIDUAL USES AS HIS OR HER CITATION. AS I LEARN AND GROW OVER TIME I AM BECOMING MORE CERTAIN THAT INFORMATION IS NOT THE ANSWER TO THE PROBLEMS OUR WORLD FACES TODAY. OUR SOCIETY IS SUFFERING FROM A LACK OF WISDOM, WHICH IS DEFINED AS THE ABILITY TO PRACTICALLY AND EMPATHETICALLY APPLY WHAT YOU KNOW IN YOUR EVERYDAY LIFE.

I have, however, found a solution to the lack. It is found in the book of Proverbs, a powerful thirty-one chapters of insight, strategy and good, plain, old-fashioned wisdom. Proverbs, found in the Judeo-Christian tradition, contain wisdom that transcends religious affiliation. If you will give Proverbs a chance, I guarantee you will know more about how to handle finances, resolve disagreements, create a happy family, run a thriving business, and be a robust part of your community than you ever thought possible. Proverbs is, simply, rich in solutions that are both practical and graceful. A lot of the problems we see today are not new—and neither is the way out of them.

Give Proverbs one month: read a chapter
a day from the Holy Bible.

Way 54

Campus Conversations

ONE OF THE MOST DIFFICULT THINGS FOR MANY PEOPLE TO DO IS TO PART IDEOLOGICAL WAYS WITH A FAMILY WHO HAS MADE DECISIONS TO BE AN ACTIVE PART OF THE SOCIETY OF YESTERDAY AND CONTINUE TO MARGINALIZE AND TRY TO SUBJUGATE OTHER PEOPLE BASED SOLELY UPON THE COLOR OF THEIR SKIN. THERE IS, HOWEVER, A GENERATION RISING WHOSE MEMBERS ARE WILLING TO TAKE WHAT, FOR THEM, IS THE UNCOMFORTABLE STEP OF OPTING-OUT OF STINKIN' THINKIN'.

Some of the most authentic and productive conversations about diversity are happening on college campuses and, in general, among the college-aged generation. A joyfully heartening number among this group of thinkers is saying NO to the jaundiced bias passed down by some of their elders, or even passed along by some of their contemporaries. Part of the reason for this is that they have grown up in a world they have never known not to be global. These young folks are building bridges across land and water, making a difference one conversation, and relationship, at a time. Bravo, GenY!

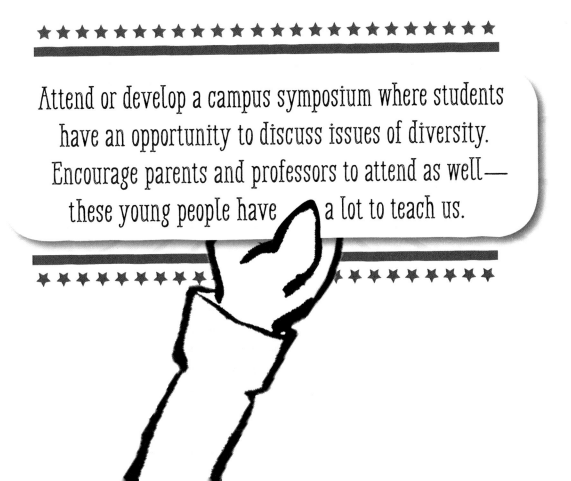

Attend or develop a campus symposium where students have an opportunity to discuss issues of diversity. Encourage parents and professors to attend as well— these young people have a lot to teach us.

Way 55

Go Deep

WE LIVE IN A SOCIETY OF HIP LABELS AND COOL BRANDS. OF PRODUCTS AND PROCEDURES THAT PROMISE TO MAKE YOU INTO THE PERFECT YOU. OF MAGAZINES AND TELEVISION SHOWS THAT PREACH ABOUT HOW TO HAVE THE RIGHT HAIR, THE BEST MANICURE, THE HOTTEST FIGURE—AND, IF THOSE THINGS AREN'T EXACTLY RIGHT? PHOTOSHOP!

If we don't measure up to these ideals, we may surely be forgiven for thinking less of ourselves, because that's exactly what we're supposed to think! Make-up companies and plastic surgeons make good profits, after all, by messing around with our self-esteem!

Worse, we often judge not only ourselves but other people based on how they conform, or do not conform, to what the fashion magazines say is in style.

It's always been my mantra that it is hard enough being me; why would I work even harder to try to be someone else? How much happier would we all be if, instead of trying to fit into someone else's model, we celebrated our own uniqueness?

How much more content would we be if we realized how necessary we are, just as we are—and that others are necessary just as they are too.

Listen to the way you think. The next time you find yourself judging yourself or someone else based on the way you/they look, check yourself. Remember that everyone has a rich and compelling story, and there's just no way to ever even guess what that story might be by how much you weigh or what designer they wear.

Way 56
Finding the Matrix

OK, SO, I'LL ADMIT IT. I AM NOT A BIG SCI-FI FAN, BUT OCCASIONALLY A FILM COMES ALONG THAT IS JUST TOO GOOD TO DISMISS MERELY BECAUSE OF ITS GENRE. SUCH WAS THE CASE OF THE FILM *THE MATRIX* WHEN IT FIRST HIT THE MARKET YEARS AGO.

The matrix, as you'll learn when you watch, is a place where people enter into a digital world of the reality of their choosing, all generated by a large supercomputer. One of my favorite exchanges in the movie is when Morpheus, played skillfully by Laurence Fishburne, says to the One/Neo, played by Keenau Reeves: "This is your last chance. After this, there is no turning back. You take the blue pill, the story ends, you wake up in your bed and believe whatever you want to believe. You take the red pill, you stay in Wonderland and I show you how deep the rabbit-hole goes." As most of us know, Neo takes the red pill, saying to Morpheus, "My eyes hurt." To which Morpheus responds, "It's because you've never used them before."

To me, that particular set piece evokes questions of racism. The reason many people don't believe that racism is still an issue is because it is not, in most instances, as overt these days as it once was. Unfortunately, however, it is still as much a part of the fabric of our society as the air we breathe. It is all around us, multi-layered, and, oh, so subtle. Indeed, some of its current power is its subtlety…like the Matrix.

View the movie *The Matrix* with a group of friends and discuss the movie's parallels with the ubiquitous nature of racism in America.

Way 57
Book Worm

PERSONALLY, I LOVE READING. SOME OF MY FAVORITE BOOKS ARE ABOUT A CULTURE I HAVEN'T YET EXPLORED—OR HAVEN'T YET EXPLORED TO MY SATISFACTION—WRITTEN BY A PERSON FROM INSIDE THAT CULTURE. SOMEONE WHO KNOWS THE CULTURE AND CAN GIVE ME INSIDE INFORMATION AND INSIGHT.

I am a big fan of TED (Technology, Entertainment and Design; *www.ted.com*). One of my favorite talks is from Nigerian Novelist, Chimamande Adichie. In her TED talk, "The Danger of a Single Story," Adichie speaks about how disturbing it was to discover the stereotypes that her roommate at an American college had about Africans—and how disturbing it was to find that she herself was harboring stereotypes about whole groups of other people.

Here's the power of reading non-American authors for me. It ope[n]
mind to the psychology of other groups of people who do not see throu[gh]
American lens. These books allow me to see a world that isn't brough[t]
focus by my assumptions and prejudices—and they reveal to me the m[...]
[i]n which those things I hold most valuable or comfortable, or even norm[al]
[p]erceived by people whose own assumptions and prejudices are very di[...]
[f]rom mine. My editor reminds me at this pass that she once attended a l[...]
[b]y Kwame Anthony Appiah, a Ghanaian-American scholar currently te[aching]
[i]n the New York University Department of Philosophy, at which he said, [in the]
[c]ourse of recommending books by African authors to the audience of [...]
white Americans: "Narcissism is not the only reason to read." There is tr[uth in]
[t]his statement on so many layers and levels!

★★★★★★★★★★★★★★★★★★★★★★★★★★★★★★★★

Start a book club where the focus is to read and discuss
books written by authors from diverse corners of the world.
And check out Adichie's Ted Talk right here:
www.ted.com/talks/chimamanda_adichie_
the_danger_of_a_single_story.

Way 58
Dude It

IN A WORLD OF CUBICLES, COMPRESSED TIME, LUNCHES AT ONE'S DESK, AND THE CONSTANT HUM AND DISTURBANCE OF TECHNOLOGY, UNPLUGGING YOURSELF AND SPENDING TIME IN THE GREAT OUTDOORS CAN BE A SANITY SAVER. I ROUTINELY ASK THE PROFESSIONALS WITH WHOM I WORK IF THEY'VE TAKEN THE TIME LATELY TO GET OUTSIDE AND SPEND SOME TIME ACTUALLY BREATHING FRESH AIR? MANY OF THEM STARE AT ME BLANKLY IN RESPONSE, FUMBLING FOR AN ANSWER. OTHERS—ACTUALLY, TOO MANY OF THEM—SPOUT THE SAME RESPONSE: "I'M TOO BUSY!" REALLY? THAT'S ONE HECK OF A TERRIBLE EXCUSE.

Working so hard that we forget to *be* seems to me a fundamental misunderstanding of the human condition. We are not, after all, called human doings, we are called human beings. In order to be our best, we must take time out to get refreshed and stop holding up our vast pool of unused sick days as if they're a badge of honor. If you want to be truly, really, authentically effective at your job, take some time off! And don't wimp out about your vacation. Push your leisure to the limit of your comfort zone. Hike the Himalayas. Swim with the dolphins. Reserve a spot at a western-style dude ranch. The end of my own personal comfort zone? That dude ranch in Texas. Horseback riding all day, cooking my evening meal over a fire and eating it under the stars, drinking "Texas rot gut" (which I understand to be extremely strong coffee) on a crisp morning on the range. I have yet to actually do this, so here's my challenge: if you take yourself on your fantasy vacation, I'll take myself on mine!

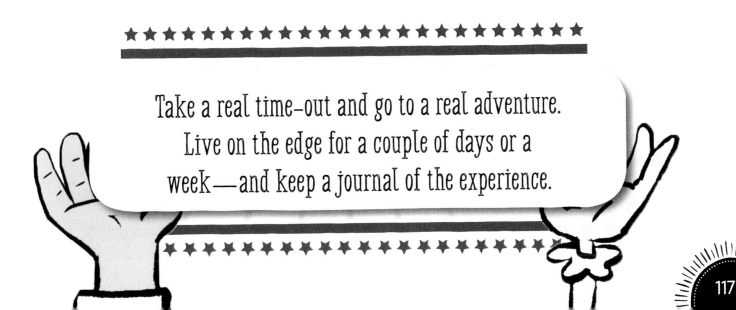

Take a real time-out and go to a real adventure.
Live on the edge for a couple of days or a
week—and keep a journal of the experience.

Way 59
Stories

WHAT'S YOUR FAVORITE NOVEL? YOUR FAVORITE THEATRICAL MOVIE? YOUR FAVORITE TV DRAMA OR COMEDY? WHY DO THESE FICTIONS RESONATE WITH YOU SO STRONGLY? CHANCES ARE THERE IS SOMETHING IN THE STORY THAT SPEAKS TO YOUR OWN STORY.

This is the beautiful part of what novelists and screenwriters and other types of artists do—they tell the stories of our culture, our society, and us in ways that reflect and explain, and thus help us to understand, the world we live in and ourselves.

Well, it isn't only artists that have stories to tell, of course. Each of us has his or her own story. Our emotions are formed and tangled up within our own personal narrative, and may, to some greater or lesser degree, impact the esteem in which we are able to hold the tale of our own lives. But here's

we all need to accept: nobody's story is better than anyone else's—simply different. Think that snobbish person with the degree fro
ious university is better than you? That's because he hasn't told yo
't want to tell you—about the bruises he suffered along the way.
omeless woman in the shelter isn't as good as you are? That's becau
know—and maybe would not immediately understand—the pro
aced that brought her to where she is.

★★★★★★★★★★★★★★★★★★★★★★★★★★★★

Embrace your own story—the loves, the sorrows, the laughs, the mistakes and the victories and the pratfalls. They are part of what has made you you. Share your story proudly. If you're not ready to shout it to the world, perhaps because you don't yet know how to tell it, purchase a blank journal and write in it every day for a month. Every human being has two basic needs: to be seen and to be heard. If you aren't ready yet for the world to hear your story, become more comfortable with it by telling it to yourself.

Way 60

A Day in the Life

FOR MANY OF US, IT IS FAR TOO EASY TO SAY WHAT WE WOULD DO IF WE WERE SOMEONE ELSE. YOUR COLLEGE ROOMMATE IS FLUNKING OUT OF HER CLASSES AND YOU MIGHT ASSUME IT'S BECAUSE SHE CAME FROM A BACKGROUND IN WHICH HER FAMILY DID NOT OR WAS UNABLE TO HELP HER DEVELOP GOOD STUDY HABITS AND TIME MANAGEMENT SKILLS, BUT REALLY WHAT SHE HASN'T HAD THE HEART TO TELL YOU IS THAT HER PARENTS ARE GETTING A DIVORCE. YOU COME ACROSS A PHOTO OF A WOMAN IN A THIRD WORLD COUNTRY WHO IS UNABLE TO FEED HER LARGE FAMILY AND YOU BELIEVE IF THAT WERE YOU, YOU WOULD HAVE LIMITED THE NUMBER OF CHILDREN YOU BIRTHED, BUT WHAT YOU DON'T KNOW IS THAT VARIOUS RESOURCES ARE UNAVAILABLE TO HER IN HER COUNTRY.

How many times have you decided what someone else ought to do based on what you believe you would do if you were in the same situation? I'm challenging you, then, to actually try it.

★ ★

Decide upon a Third World country that is of interest to you and truly immerse yourself in it through study. Learn all you can about how an average person in that country lives on a day-to-day basis. Now, imagine you are that person, living in that country, both enjoying its culture and enduring its hardships. How would your life be different? What opportunities would be available or not available for you? Walk a few miles in someone else's shoes, because it's only after you've done that that you can talk about how sore your feet are.

AS OF THIS WRITING, THE UNITED STATES OF AMERICA HAS THE LARGEST NUMBER OF INCARCERATED CITIZENS OF ANY NATION ON THE PLANET. THIS IS NOT A CRITIQUE, IT'S A FACT. WHEN I FIRST HEARD THIS TRUTH, IT TOOK A WHILE TO SINK IN. HOW COULD IT BE THAT THE RICHEST, MOST DIVERSE AND MOST TECHNOLOGICALLY ADVANCED DEMOCRATIC NATION IN THE WORLD WAS LOCKING UP MORE OF HER CITIZENS THAN ANY OTHER PLACE ON EARTH?

You want an even more astonishing fact? The majority of those incarcerated are Latino and African-American men.

The complex nature of incarceration in the U.S. requires study. Knee-jerk reactions on either side of an issue aren't ever helpful. But here are some specific questions we need to ask in this particular situation:

Why, if the U.S. accounts for only 5% of the world's population, does it account for 22% of the world's prison population?

Why do African-Americans make up only 12% of the U.S. population, but 44% of the country's prison population?

Why are Native American youths three times as likely to be held in juvenile detention facilities as white youths?

Why are Latinos imprisoned at the rate of almost one and a half times the rate for whites?

Are Blacks, Native Americans, and Latinos that much more prone to criminality than whites... Or are there other factors that contribute to such disparity in the U.S. prison population? Factors such as the difference between minimum sentences for possession of powder cocaine, which is primarily used by white drug users, and crack cocaine, which is primarily used by Black drug users?

Why does it take possession of 100x the amount of powder cocaine as crack cocaine to receive the same prison sentence?

Read Michelle Alexander's book *The New Jim Crow* and gather a group of ethnically diverse people to have a conversation about this powerful book and the issue with which it grapples.

Way 62

Step Up to the Plate

BELIEVE, OF COURSE, IN FREEDOM OF SPEECH—LIKE MOST AMERICANS,
I'M A BIG FAN OF THE FIRST AMENDMENT.

But I also believe that hate speech is a thing apart from that freedom, and therefore it should be checked. If someone has the boldness to put witlessness on display, then they need to be ready to receive the rebuke that comes back at them. Racism, sexism, xenophobia and the like come in many forms—from a podium where a politician shouts out dog-whistle words to your friend at the office holiday party who thinks it's just fine to make what he thinks is just a funny crack at the expense of his female co-workers.

What do you say to these people? What have you said when you've heard such talk? Do you say something to them or do you just let it go for fear of being seen as touchy, or oversensitive, or too "politically correct"?

I've always said there are two kinds of people when it comes to this sort of scenario. First, there are the velvet-glove folks. There is no malicious intent behind what velvet-glove folks say; they speak from pure ignorance and they're ready to learn if only someone would call them on their errors.

Then there are the 2x4 folks meaning, in my view, that even if you hit them over the head with a 2x4 they won't change their ways.

In the end, it is simply time to stop allowing stupidity and bigotry to walk right into the center of the room and have its say. When that happens, it is up to the other people in the room to make sure that it knows it is most unwelcome. And, when those other people in the room include you, it is, indeed, then up to you to be a part of telling the speaker that his or her language is inappropriate and unacceptable.

★★★★★★★★★★★★★★★★★★★★★★★★★★★★

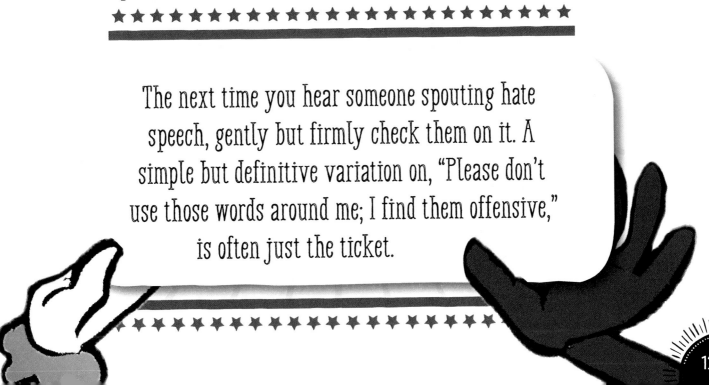

The next time you hear someone spouting hate speech, gently but firmly check them on it. A simple but definitive variation on, "Please don't use those words around me; I find them offensive," is often just the ticket.

Way 63

Culture Club

THE SOONER WE BEGIN TEACHING OUR CHILDREN ABOUT OTHER CULTURES, THE SOONER THEIR CURIOSITY WILL BE TWEAKED—AND THE SOONER THEY'LL BECOME CULTURALLY COMPETENT.

By nurturing our kids' natural curiosity, we help to make life-long learners out of them. But I want to make clear that cultural competence is no longer an option, something fun but extracurricular; in our age of globalization it is a necessity if we want our kids to have a competitive advantage.

Years ago, when our own children were small, my awesome wife, Barbara, started a Culture Club at their school. Each month, the kids chose a new country to study. My wife, along with other volunteers, arranged for a speaker who could represent that country to come and talk to the kids about its history, geography, and folk traditions, and she created an ethnic menu around its cuisine that the kids then prepared and dined upon at the gathering. The kids *loved* it! And the parents? Most of them, for the first couple of months, would just drop their kids off to attend the club's meeting but, in short order, the parents began to stay for the presentations and meals as well, creating a standing-room-only situation. She soon had to find a larger venue for her meetings.

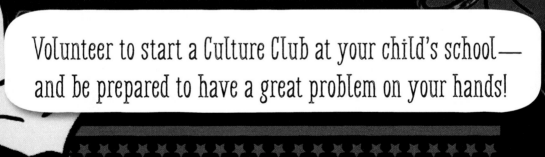

Volunteer to start a Culture Club at your child's school—and be prepared to have a great problem on your hands!

Way 64

Clip 'n' Send

NOT SO VERY MANY YEARS AGO MY LATE BROTHER-FROM-ANOTHER-MOTHER, RICK WILSON, AND I TOOK A ROAD TRIP TO A CONFERENCE IN A MID-WEST STATE. WE WERE ABOUT THREE HOURS INTO THE TRIP AND IT WAS TIME TO REFUEL. WE DECIDED TO DO SO IN A LITTLE TOWN THAT SEEMED TO CONSIST PRIMARILY OF A MCDONALDS AND, WELL, THE GAS STATION. IN THE CAR RICK AND I HAD BEEN LISTENING TO OUR FAVORITE ENTERTAINER OF ALL TIME, MICHAEL JACKSON, AND WE HAD BEEN ROCKIN' PRETTY HARD, BUT WHEN WE GOT OUT OF THE CAR TO GET GAS AND SNACKS... SCREECH! IT WAS LIKE A NEEDLE SCRATCHING A RECORD RIGHT THROUGH THE BEST PART OF THE SONG.

People were staring at us, giving us the oddest looks. The air seemed to be sucked right out of the atmosphere. You would have thought that we were from another planet—but we were just a multi-ethnic pair, and the people in this town were not ready for us.

This was a community that was stuck in a time warp.

One of the easiest ways to find out if your community has moved with the times is to look at your local newspaper. Do the stories feature people that all look the same, or does the paper include stories about the community's ethnic populations as well? How are the stories weighted? Are ethnic minorities covered in ways that celebrate that culture, or reinforce negative stereotypes?

In order for any media to stay relevant these days, it must be culturally connected—and you can help your local media stay current. Cut out articles from your local newspaper that relate to diversity issues over a period of thirty days. At the end of this period of time, do an assessment of how culturally aware your local paper is. If the coverage of diversity issues or your town's communities of color is sparse, write to the paper's editor and make some suggestions about content.

Way 65
Listen and Learn

THERE ARE CERTAIN WORDS IN THE ENGLISH LANGUAGE THAT HAVE A LOT OF BAGGAGE ASSOCIATED WITH THEM. ONE OF THOSE WORDS IS DIVERSITY.

Often those with conservative views try to make it a partisan—almost dirty—word, attaching it to some touchy-feely perception of liberalism as an ideology based on a lot of group hugs. Not that I have a problem with group hugs, but that's not what either liberalism or diversity are all about.

Let's get the definition of diversity right! The root of the word is diverse, an adjective meaning, simply, showing a great deal of variety. The noun, diversity, has a couple of pertinent meanings.

First, it refers to the state of being diverse. When you're talking about the modern-day population of the United States, saying that it is diverse is objectively accurate.

The second meaning of diversity revolves around the concept of inclusion, meaning that someone who supports diversity seeks to include people of different religions, cultures, colors, genders, sexual orientations, and socioeconomic groups in the conversation, on whatever level that conversation is happening—in the workplace, in politics, in the marketplace, or in our own personal lives.

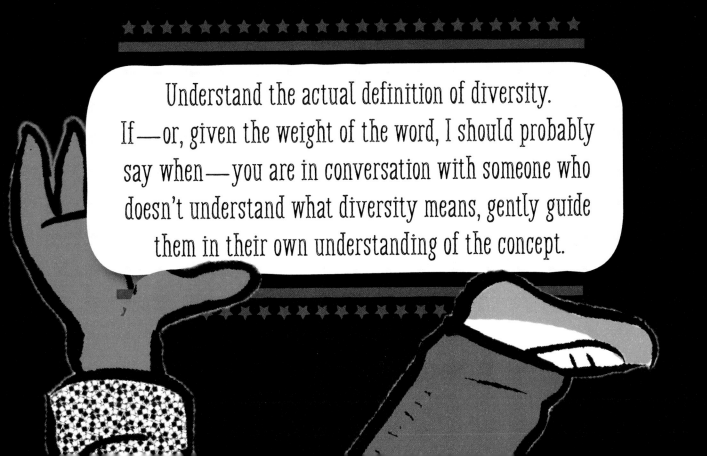

Understand the actual definition of diversity.
If—or, given the weight of the word, I should probably say when—you are in conversation with someone who doesn't understand what diversity means, gently guide them in their own understanding of the concept.

Way 66

WBIAS-TV

T'S RARE, BUT IT STILL HAPPENS IN THE 21ST CENTURY THAT THERE ARE SOME COMMERCIALS, TV SHOWS, AND OTHER FORMS OF VISUAL ENTERTAINMENT THAT MAKE IT SEEM AS IF THE WORLD STILL LOOKS LIKE THE CAST OF *LEAVE IT TO BEAVER*. LET ME ASSURE YOU—THAT'S NO LONGER HOW THE WORLD LOOKS. IT ACTUALLY NEVER DID REALLY LOOK THAT WAY, BUT NOW THAT WE ARE MOVING TO A PLACE IN OUR SOCIETY WHERE WE ARE INCLUDING ALL MEMBERS OF OUR BEAUTIFULLY DIVERSE MOSAIC IN OUR MARKETPLACES OF BOTH GOODS AND IDEAS, WELL... THAT OLD LOOK REALLY DOESN'T CUT IT. WHEN ADVERTISERS AND ENTERTAINERS GET IT WRONG, IT FEELS AS IF THEY ARE VERY MUCH OUT OF TOUCH. THE TAPESTRY OF LIFE IS NOT HOMOGENEOUS, SO WHY SHOULD PROGRAMMING BE?

Now, before you get on your historical bandwagon to tell me that there are times where certain topics, in order to be addressed with historical accuracy, must present a more monolithic cast of characters: yes, yes... I get that. I've enjoyed Jane Austen as much as the next person, and I, too, would be rattled if, suddenly, Kitty Bennet were being played by an actress of color. But I am just as rattled when, among even supporting cast members—the surgeon, the nosy next-door neighbor, the plumber, the teacher—there is not even an attempt at diversity.

The point is that heterogeneous programming makes sense. One of the reasons it makes sense is pure economics, i.e., dollars and cents. Diversity sells. And smart companies know it. That's how the discipline of multi-ethnic marketing emerged. The world is not the same as it was fifty years ago, and neither are we. The entertainment we are offered ought to reflect that.

★★★★★★★★★★★★★★★★★★★★★★★★★★★

Watch a sampling of various programs. As you watch TV ask yourself if the cast is culturally and ethnically representative of society. Are the ethnic characters written or performed in ways that promote stereotype? What opportunities do you see where the commercial or show could have been cast in a way to make it more representative of modern-day America?

★★★★★★★★★★★★★★

Way 67
Walking The Talk

THERE ARE TWO ROCK SOLID WAYS TO SEE HOW SERIOUS AN ORGA-
NIZATION IS ABOUT THEIR DIVERSITY AND INCLUSION INITIATIVE,
KNOWN WITHIN THE MARKETPLACE AS THE D&I.

First way is to ascertain from what level the D&I is being led. If it is being
led at the specialist level, or an even lower management level, this tells
me that diversity and inclusion is still considered "parsley on the plate"
by the company. That is, management thinks such an initiative looks
good, but isn't really necessary to the efficient and profitable functioning
of the company.

Second way is to know the budget the company has assigned to design and
implement the initiative. If the budget is not a percentage commensurate to

other operationally core items of the organization, then the organization is not yet to the point where they are serious about D&I.

Many companies have great intentions when it comes to D&I, and they are ambitious when they begin their diversity initiative, but I have found too few that actually stick with it, measure it, and track its results. Now, assuming your company even has a diversity plan—and many still do not—it will be worth your while to find out how the plan is being implemented. What happens when various goals or objectives aren't met? Does your organization have a Diversity Advisory Council? If so, who is on it? Who holds whom accountable to make sure that the work is actually getting done? A diversity and inclusion plan is no longer a nice corporate extra; it's a strategic document that should be an integral part of any proactive business-planning process.

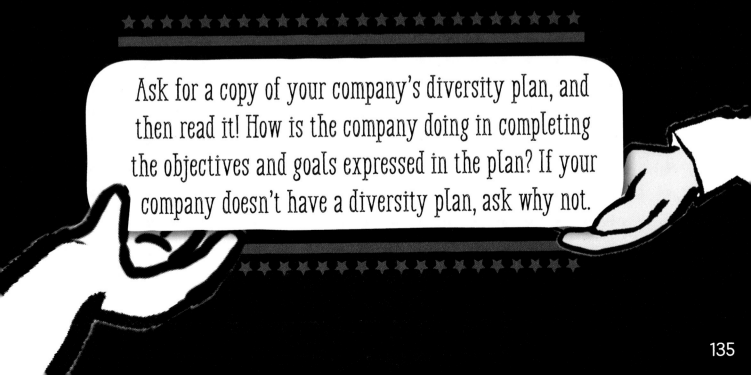

Ask for a copy of your company's diversity plan, and then read it! How is the company doing in completing the objectives and goals expressed in the plan? If your company doesn't have a diversity plan, ask why not.

Way 68
Stinkin' Thinkin'

I WAS OUT TO DINNER WITH A LARGE GROUP OF PEOPLE AND WE WERE DISCUSSING A NEW ACCOUNTANT ONE OF THEM HAD RECENTLY HIRED. SO QUICKLY THAT IT MADE MY HEAD SPIN, ONE OF THE WOMEN SAID, "OH, BE CAREFUL ABOUT TRUSTING YOUR BOOKKEEPING TO THOSE PEOPLE—EVERYONE KNOWS THOSE PEOPLE ARE VERY BAD WITH MONEY."

It was all I could do to get my breath back before I—gently, gently—corrected her. But the episode left me thinking: How had this woman formed the opinion she'd blurted out to us at the dinner table? How had it become so engrained in her mind as a truth? What experience had she extrapolated to believe it so wholeheartedly?

And then I thought: How many of us carry with us secret biases? Opinions formed and carried with us so strongly or for so long that we are unaware of the core fallacy of them?

"Be careful about doing business with one of those people." "What was she thinking? She married one of those people." "Be careful about going to that part of town, there are a lot of those people that live there." Have you ever thought something negative about someone, or several people, just because, in your mind, they belong to *those people*? I have. And I feel blessed that I have been able to catch myself, do my homework, rethink and correct myself. I've learned that the moment those pronouns step into the description of any individual, stupidity is not far behind.

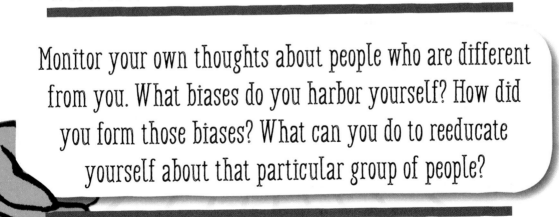

Monitor your own thoughts about people who are different from you. What biases do you harbor yourself? How did you form those biases? What can you do to reeducate yourself about that particular group of people?

Way 69
Tchotchkes

A BUTTON. AN ASHTRAY. A MUSIC BOX. AT FIRST BLUSH, THESE ITEMS SEEM INSIGNIFICANT, EVEN TRIVIAL, ONLY TCHOTCHKES—UNTIL YOU HEAR THE STORY BEHIND THE ITEM. THE BUTTON IS FROM YOUR GRANDFATHER'S MILITARY UNIFORM THAT HE WORE IN A BATTLE ALMOST A CENTURY AGO. THE ASHTRAY WAS USED ON THE SET OF A FILM BACK IN THE 1920S THAT YOUR AUNTIE DESIGNED—SHE WAS *THE* DESIGNER OF CRYSTAL CHANDELIERS IN HER DAY. THE MUSIC BOX HAD ONCE BELONGED TO YOUR GREAT-GRANDMAMA, BROUGHT FROM HER NATIVE COUNTRY AS A LITTLE GIRL—IT WAS THE ONLY TOY THAT SURVIVED THE LONG JOURNEY.

Most families collect photos, letters, silverware or other artifacts passed down through the generations. These are precious items of family history they hold dear. The artifact, however, is only as precious as the story behind it. Set aside a moment or two of everyday time to pass along the stories of those objects to the next generation of your family, and even your friends who might find them interesting. Next time you dust that music box, tell your son its story, so that he too will know and appreciate his ancestor. Next time your daughter is in your office, share the reason you keep that button on a tray on your desk, so that she will also be inspired by your grandfather's courage—after all, he's her great-grandfather! Don't let the stories slip away from the generations that will follow.

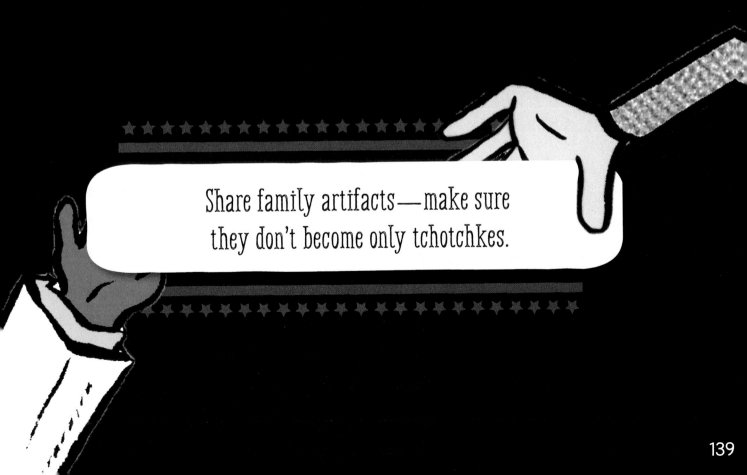

Share family artifacts—make sure they don't become only tchotchkes.

Way 70

Double Speak

TIME FOR A CONFESSION: ENGLISH IS MY FIRST LANGUAGE, AND I KNOW JUST ENOUGH GERMAN AND KOREAN TO BE DANGEROUS. LANGUAGES FASCINATE ME AND I ALWAYS WISH I WERE MORE MULTI-LINGUAL THAN I AM—WHICH IS WHY I'M CURRENTLY DEEPLY IMMERSED IN MY STUDY OF SPANISH.

My kids have an advantage over me in the language department. My wife and I raised them in a school district where there were some seventy languages spoken by their classmates, representing a full sixty-eight countries. It was an amazingly rich environment in which to be educated. Language is the key to a people's story; for what better way to understand their history, their victories, their hurts, and their struggles than to hear those experiences expressed in their own words? As we become ever more globalized as a society—and the boundaries of the marketplace continue, accordingly, to expand—what better advantage can you give your kids than to help them acquire the skill to speak at least one other language?

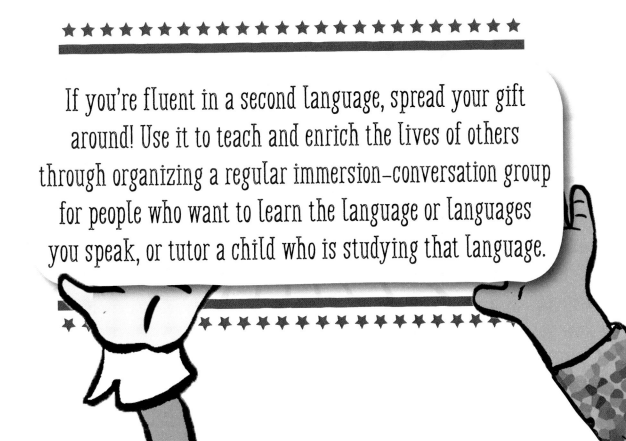

If you're fluent in a second language, spread your gift around! Use it to teach and enrich the lives of others through organizing a regular immersion-conversation group for people who want to learn the language or languages you speak, or tutor a child who is studying that language.

Way 71

A Collaborative Economy

A FRIEND TELLS THE STORY OF THE SMALL, MOM-AND-POP GROCERY STORE WHERE HER FAMILY BOUGHT MOST OF THEIR GROCERIES WHEN SHE WAS GROWING UP. THIS PARTICULAR STORE WAS LOCATED IN HER CITY'S LITTLE ITALY, IN THE MIDST OF A LARGE ITALIAN POPULATION, AND IT STOCKED ALL THE SPECIALTY INGREDIENTS THAT EVERY ITALIAN HOME COOK CONSIDERED STAPLES. WHEN SHE VISITS HER HOMETOWN THESE DAYS, SHE'S STILL ABLE TO SHOP AT THE SAME LITTLE GROCERY STORE, STILL RUN BY THE NEXT GENERATION OF THE SAME FAMILY. EVEN IF THE NEIGHBORHOOD IS NO LONGER ETHNICALLY HOMOGENEOUS AND THOSE ONCE-ESOTERIC INGREDIENTS—POLENTA AND PROSCIUTTO, AS EXAMPLES—ARE MORE MAINSTREAM, THE LITTLE STORE HAS RETAINED ITS REPUTATION FOR SELLING ONLY THE HIGHEST QUALITY ITEMS. "I DON'T KNOW WHAT WOULD HAVE HAPPENED TO THAT GROCERY STORE WHEN THE NEIGHBORHOOD WAS GENTRIFIED IF IT STILL HAD TO DEPEND ON A STRICTLY ITALIAN CLIENTELE!" SHE TOLD ME.

When our goal is a thriving, diverse community, this is the place where the rubber meets the road: the local economy. It is nearly impossible to have that kind of a community unless all the neighborhoods—and all the people within them—are thriving equally. In order to live in the sort of healthy community we all deserve, we must support the products and services of the diverse entrepreneurs who make up our towns and cities. The whole of our local economies is only as strong as their weakest link; your shopping habits can do a great deal to help the vibrancy of the whole.

Read the book *Our Black Year: One Family's Quest to Buy Black in America's Racially Divided Economy* by Maggie Anderson. Make a pledge to spend your dollars with diversity.

Way 72
Flip Flop

·····•••••◦•◦●◉●◦•◦•••·····

THE PHRASE "WHITE MAN'S BURDEN" FIRST ENTERED OUR LEXICON IN 1899, THROUGH A POEM OF THE SAME TITLE WRITTEN BY RUDYARD KIPLING AS A JUSTIFICATION FOR COLONIALIZATION—TO PROMOTE THE IDEA OF EMPIRE, AND THAT IN IMPOSING EUROCENTRIC INDUSTRIALIZATION THE WORLD WOULD BECOME CIVILIZED.

The 1995 movie of this name, starring Harry Belafonte and John Travolta, flips the premise and asks what life in the United States might be if the rules society imposed were flipped—if Blacks were the members of the wealthy establishment and whites were a disadvantaged minority group.

The first time I saw this movie it really tripped me out. Though I have thought about what the reversal of roles in society between the African-American man and the Euro-American man might mean, I have never really understood what seeing it would look like. Interestingly, the movie was written and directed by Desmond Nakano, a Japanese-American man, who brings his own perspective as an American person of color to the film, and to the quest for justice that is its premise.

Rent the movie *White Man's Burden* and watch it with a group of friends and/or family. Put on a pot of coffee or pour another glass of wine because, when the film is over, I guarantee the discussion will be lively and long!

Way 73
Make Inroads

EXPOSING OUR YOUNG PEOPLE TO A WIDE VARIETY OF CAREER OPTIONS AND THEN MENTORING THEM SO THEY ARE ABLE TO FIND ONE THAT BEST SUITS AND SATISFIES THEM ARE TWO TASKS ALL OF US ADULTS ARE RESPONSIBLE FOR CARRYING OUT. I CAN'T COUNT THE NUMBER OF FAVORS I'VE CALLED IN OR LETTERS I'VE WRITTEN ON BEHALF OF MY OWN AND OTHER YOUNGSTERS TO HELP THEM FIND A FIT IN AN INDUSTRY IN WHICH THEY WANT TO SPEND THEIR CAREER.

In 1970, however, a man named Frank C. Carr noticed that there weren't a lot of ethnically diverse employees among corporate management in the US, and he set out to change that. Starting in Chicago, with just a handful of companies backing him, and only seventeen college-aged interns, he grew his brainchild, Inroads, to where it is now, in partnership with over two hundred corporations, serving nearly two thousand young interns!

Help a young person get plugged into the career of her or his dreams. Find out if your company is a contributor to Inroads. If it isn't, take it upon yourself to enlist their help to grow this remarkable organization and help them to continue their important work. You can find them at *www.inroads.org*.

Way 74

Vision Casting

VISION CASTING IS A TECHNIQUE OR PRACTICE THAT IS FAMILIAR TO MOST ENTREPRENEURS. IT IS A SIMPLE, PRACTICAL, AND REALLY FUN EXERCISE IN WHICH THE ENTREPRENEUR COMMUNICATES THE BIG PICTURE OF WHAT HER COMPANY IS GOING TO LOOK LIKE IN THE FUTURE: WHAT WILL IT SELL? WHAT SERVICE(S) WILL IT OFFER? WHO WILL BE ITS CUSTOMERS? WHAT ARE THE SPECIFIC BENEFITS AND RESULTS HER COMPANY WILL DELIVER TO HER AND HER EMPLOYEES?

My suggestion is that we borrow this exercise from the entrepreneurs and use it more broadly, applying it to our very lives, and to the diversity we hope to bring into them. What are your hopes and dreams? What are you passionate about, and why? What is the world that you envision in your heart of hearts? Do you want to attend a service at a church where, though you don't belong, you've heard a heavenly choir when you walk by on a Sunday morning? Do you want to start a service club in your school or at your company? Do you want to finally take that long-dreamed-of trip to India? What keeps you looking to the future, motivated and ready to go?

These are questions that people rarely ask themselves. But, like the woman who is starting her own business, if we have no idea what we want our own world to look like, we have very little chance of actually living in the world of our dreams.

★★★★★★★★★★★★★★★★★★★★★★★★★★★

Spend an evening with yourself, thinking about your vision for your future. Write down half a dozen concrete ways you'd like your world to improve. Commit your dreams to paper so you have tangible evidence of them, then tuck that list away so you can refer to it when you repeat this exercise, every few months, to see how your goals and objectives are coming to fruition—and what new goals you can add to your list to replace or expand on the ones you've already met.

★★★★★★★★★★★★★★

Way 75

Diversity on a Page

ONE OF THE MOST IMPORTANT THINGS WE, AS PARENTS, CAN DO WITH OUR YOUNG CHILDREN IS TO FOSTER IN THEM A LOVE OF READING. MOST OF US KNOW THIS AND WE TAKE REAL PLEASURE IN BUYING PICTURE BOOKS FOR THEM WHEN THEY'RE YOUNG, AND CUDDLING UP WITH THEM IN OUR LAPS TO ENJOY A FAVORITE ONE OR TWO BEFORE BED TIME. AS THEY GROW UP, IT BECOMES A PARTICULAR DELIGHT TO SHARE WITH THEM THE BOOKS THAT WE LOVED WHEN WE WERE THEIR AGE—STORIES THAT ENGROSSED US, AUTHORS THAT INSPIRED US.

Take a moment, however, to think about the books your children read. Do they reflect the glorious mosaic of the world's stories, or do they box your kids into one small part of the picture? Do they merely reflect the place in the world he or she already inhabits, or do they ignite his imagination, stir her interest in, and empathy for, all the people who make up the world?

Look through your child's library or, if you're not a parent yourself, through the library of a child in your life. What titles are there? What worlds do the characters inhabit? What are their ethnicities, socio-economic groups, how do they self-identify? What are their cultural conventions? If you find that the characters in your kid's stories could paint a more colorful, diverse rainbow, check out weneeddiversebooks.org/where-to-find-diverse-books/. Help your kids cultivate a library that encompasses the whole, beautiful world!

Way 76
Crash a Party

CRASH, THE 2004 MOVIE WRITTEN AND DIRECTED BY PAUL HAGGIS, IS ONE OF THE MOST HONEST AND PENETRATING FILMS ON THE TOPIC OF RACE AND ETHNICITY EVER MADE. WHEN I FIRST SAW IT, I SAT THERE FOR A FULL FIFTEEN MINUTES AFTER IT WAS OVER BECAUSE I WAS, QUITE FRANKLY, STUNNED. HERE'S THE DEAL, PEOPLE: UNLESS WE DEAL WITH SOME OF THE HARSH REALITIES OF THE SOCIETAL CANCER OF RACISM, WE'LL NEVER BECOME WHAT IS POSSIBLE FOR US TO BECOME—WE WILL BE LESSER AS INDIVIDUALS, OUR COMMUNITIES WON'T BE WHOLE, AND OUR COUNTRY WON'T BE AS GREAT AS WE'D ALL LIKE TO BELIEVE IT CAN BE.

Throw a *Crash* party. Gather a multi-ethnic group of friends and family and watch the movie together. When it's over, have a conversation about inter-racial (across different groups) and intra-racial (within the same group) conflict—but don't discuss only the conflict, discuss solutions. You might think that the problems are too big, or you're too small to find ways to resolve these long-standing clashes, but you'd be wrong. The solutions aren't going to come along on their own; they're going to come from people who care about solving the problems. So get some people together and start thinking, and, even more important, talking.

Way 77

Vote with Your Dollars

WHEN WE MAKE A PURCHASE—ANY PURCHASE—WE ARE TACITLY GIVING OUR APPROVAL TO THE ENTITY THAT HAS MANUFACTURED THE GOODS WE ARE ACQUIRING OR HAS PROVIDED THE SERVICES WE ARE SEEKING. THE FOOD AT OUR FAVORITE RESTAURANT IS DELICIOUS, AND THIS IS WHAT WE ARE TELLING THE CHEF WHEN WE CHOOSE TO SPEND OUR MONEY THERE. THE CLOTHING FROM A PARTICULAR DESIGNER COMES IN COLORS AND STYLES WE LOVE, AND ALMOST NEVER FAILS TO FIT US BEAUTIFULLY, AND WE TELL THAT DESIGNER WE APPRECIATE HIS ARTISTRY BY PURCHASING HIS OR HER BRAND. OUR ACCOUNTANT IS HONEST, ACCURATE, AND ON TIME, AND WE TELL HER WE VALUE THE QUALITY OF HER WORK EVERY TIME WE PICK UP THE PHONE TO MAKE OUR MONTHLY OR QUARTERLY OR ANNUAL APPOINTMENT TO HAVE OUR BOOKWORK DONE.

It's important to understand what we are telling a business when we buy a product or service is that we approve of the way they do business—be even if we don't actually approve, this is still the message we send when w over our money to them. Does Corporation X pay its female employe the same scale that they pay their male employees? If pay equity is imp to you, as it is to most of us, then you could send a powerful messag company about altering their pay policy. Does your building manag discriminate against prospective tenants based on their ethnic backgr Does the hotel you've booked for your upcoming vacation belong to a corporation that regularly donates to groups or politicians who supp promote discriminatory practices? By giving businesses your hard-e dollars, you tacitly approve of their policies.

★★★★★★★★★★★★★★★★★★★★★★★★★★★

Become a conscious consumer. Research the background of the companies you do business with. Make sure the corporate values behind the products you buy and the services you use mesh well with the human values you most esteem.

Way 78

Post It & Place It

HOW DO YOU KEEP UP WITH ALL THE GOOD THINGS THAT ARE HAPPENING IN YOUR COMMUNITY? I'VE DISCOVERED THAT TOO OFTEN WE MISS EVENTS THAT MIGHT HAVE INTERESTED US, ONLY BECAUSE THERE ISN'T A HUB OR OVERALL COMMUNITY CALENDAR TO KEEP US IN THE KNOW. YOUR CHURCH MAY HAVE A VIBRANT ACTIVITY CALENDAR, BUT ARE ITS EVENTS POSTED TO YOUR TOWN'S WEB SITE CALENDAR? YOUR CHILD'S SCHOOL MIGHT BE HOSTING A TERRIFIC SPEAKER, BUT IS THAT EVENT PROMOTED OUTSIDE OF THE SCHOOL COMMUNITY? IN OTHER WORDS, IS THERE A CENTRAL, DESTINATION CALENDAR OF EVENTS WHERE ANYONE WITHIN YOUR COMMUNITY, AS WELL AS VISITORS AND TOURISTS, CAN GO TO PLAN THEIR LEISURE TIME AND TAKE BEST ADVANTAGE OF ALL YOUR TOWN OR CITY OR REGION HAS TO OFFER?

This is an important consideration because, again, too often events are promoted only to an immediate audience. My question is: Why should members of other denominations miss out when your church is hosting a wonderful gospel choir? Why shouldn't the whole community have the opportunity to watch the local Native American tribe perform seasonal dances? Having an active, dynamic, and diversity-oriented calendar is another step in the right direction for the community that is serious about really being an active and dynamic community. Community, after all, doesn't happen on the decks in our backyard—it happens on our front porches and on our streets, one wave, one hello at a time. It's tough to stay informed, however, about which porch, so to speak, the community is gathering at unless someone commits to making sure that the details of the who-what-when-where-and-why get out to the public.

★ ★

If your community doesn't already have one, create a web site—and/or a central display area—where groups and organizations can post notices of upcoming events and activities. If your community does have such a hub, good for you—contribute to it, check it to make sure it is as inclusive as you think it is, and support the events and activities promoted there by attending them!

Way 79

Brown Baggin' It

THERE IS A VOLUNTEER AT YOUR COUNTY HISTORICAL SOCIETY WHO CAN TELL YOU ABOUT HOW THE NATIONAL MOVEMENT FOR CIVIL RIGHTS MANIFESTED IN YOUR TOWN. THERE IS WOMAN WHOSE LAW PRACTICE HAS LONG REVOLVED AROUND AFFIRMATIVE ACTION CASES. THERE IS A HIGH SCHOOL-AGED GIRL WHO JUST ATTENDED A MULTI-CULTURAL ARTS CAMP AND SHE CAN TELL YOU WHY IT WAS A GREAT EXPERIENCE.

Among the ways to help communities get smarter about what's going on locally around the issues of diversity, Brown Bag Discussions are most effective. These are a series of informal talks that can be relatively easy and inexpensive to set up. Schedule your discussions to take place over the lunch hour, and ask everyone to brown bag their own meal. Then find a gathering place—a board room, a high school auditorium—and some experts who live around or in your area. Agree on a fee, if there is to be one, and schedule them to come in and talk to your group.

What sort of experts should you engage? Folks who have a strong track record in their area, as well as just regular folks who have unique stories to tell and perspectives to share. When you're choosing your presenters, keep in mind that you really shouldn't pick speakers who will be noncontroversial. It isn't a requirement that everyone in your audience has to agree with what the speaker has to say—indeed, the search to find speakers who *aren't provocative is one of the greatest disablers of productive conversation.*

Ask your company or organization to sponsor a lunchtime Brown Bag Series, and step up to act as the organizer! You don't have to have one every week of the year—start small, with a series of four or six, and then grow!

Way 80

Theatre of Testimony

THEATRE HAS BEEN AN IMPORTANT PART OF MY LIFE FOR A LONG, LONG TIME. I'VE RARELY PASSED UP AN OPPORTUNITY TO SEE A PRODUCTION, AND I'VE EVEN BEEN IN QUITE A FEW IN MY TIME TOO. I LOVE THE IMMEDIACY OF THE HUMAN CONNECTION THE THEATER OFFERS, AND THE POWER IT HAS TO TRANSFORM AND TO EVEN TRANSPORT AN AUDIENCE TO ANOTHER PLACE, SPACE AND TIME. OCCASIONALLY, MY WIFE, BARBARA, AND I HEAD TO NEW YORK TO SEE A SHOW OR TWO, BUT I MUST SAY THAT YOU DON'T HAVE TO TRAVEL TO AMERICA'S THEATRICAL HUB, BROADWAY, TO SEE GREAT SHOWS—LOCAL AND COMMUNITY THEATRE CAN OFFER THE SAME TRANSFORMATIVE EXPERIENCE.

Recently I was introduced to a type of theater that is new to me—Theatre of Testimony. This introduction was by way of a play by a friend of mine, playwright and professor Stephanie Sandberg, called Lines. It was performed by a group of local community actors, and explored the role that ethnicity, race, and racism play in my hometown of Grand Rapids, Michigan. It dealt with the subject from a localized perspective and was probably one of the best pieces of theatre I have ever seen. After the show, there was a community dialogue that I, and my late buddy, Rick Wilson, facilitated. At times the after-theater discussion was tense, but everyone there had a heart and the inclination to understand, learn, and grow.

★ ★

How powerful would it be to see what other young people could do with this genre of theatre? If you are a parent, educator, or some other interested and invested party, why not encourage your local or community theater group to create a piece of their own that explores ethnicity from your local perspective. You might be surprised what the young folks have to teach you.

★ ★

Way 81
A Foreign Language

I BELIEVE THAT ONE OF THE MAIN REASONS THAT MOST PEOPLE ARE UNCOMFORTABLE SPEAKING ABOUT ISSUES OF RACE AND ETHNICITY IS SIMPLY BECAUSE THERE AREN'T MANY PLACES WHERE YOU CAN. IT OCCURRED TO ME THAT, IN FACT, THE DISCUSSION AROUND THESE ISSUES, ESPECIALLY IN AMERICA, HAS ITS OWN LANGUAGE, WITH ITS OWN CHARACTERISTICS, FOUNDATIONS AND LEXICON. PEOPLE OFTEN STUMBLE WHEN TRYING TO COMMUNICATE THEIR IDEAS, THOUGHTS, OR PASSIONS BECAUSE THEY DON'T YET KNOW THE LANGUAGE—AND I CAN UNDERSTAND BEING SHY OF SAYING THE WRONG THING; HECK, ALL OF US HAVE THAT DUBIOUS GIFT, FROM TIME TO TIME.

What I can't understand is giving up on the conversation just because you're not yet fluent in the language. If I had to move to a different country, say Brazil, I would have to learn to speak Portuguese. Certainly I would stumble, conjugate verbs incorrectly, and maybe even unintentionally insult someone, but I would have to try.

Spend some time studying the various theories of diversity, equity, inclusion, and cultural competency. One resource is the book *Positive Organizing in a Global Society: Understanding and Engaging Differences for Capacity Building and Inclusion*, essays edited by Laura Morgan Roberts and Lynn Perry Wooten. I was honored to be asked to contribute an essay as well!

Way 82
Stop and Listen

A CRITICALLY IMPORTANT COMPONENT OF ANY COMMUNITY IS THE FAITH COMMUNITY, AND THE MEN AND WOMEN WHO LEAD IT AND HELP GUIDE THE MORAL COMPASS OF OUR WORLD. ONE OF THE LAST FRONTIERS, IN MY OPINION, FOR OUR FAITH LEADERS IS FOR THEM TO SPEAK OUT ON THE ISSUES OF BIGOTRY, PREJUDICE, AND RACISM.

In many faith gatherings around the world, racism is the elephant in the room, the subject we gloss over. We can talk about almost anything else, but if the subject of bigotry arises, almost invariably someone promptly attempts to refocus the conversation. I can't understand why more congregations don't encourage substantive conversations around this topic as it is foundational to the principles of love, understanding, and compassion that underscore not just the Christian tradition, but the traditions of all the world's great religions.

I suspect that one of the other key reasons that some faith communities refuse to address issues of race and racism from the pulpit is because they are afraid that it will make their larger givers uncomfortable, and might even cause them to find another place to worship. This fear, in itself, is one more reason we need a faith perspective on these core issues that have plagued our society for centuries. To whom much is given much is required. Selah.

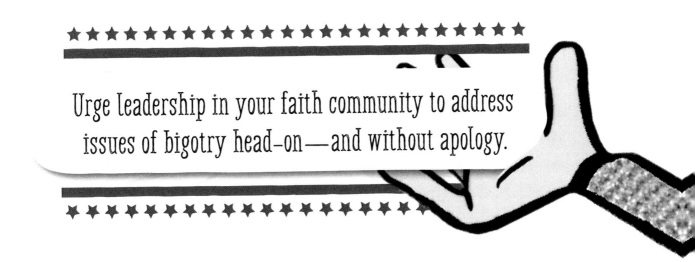

★ ★

Urge leadership in your faith community to address issues of bigotry head-on—and without apology.

★ ★

Way 83

Cool City

I REMEMBER HEARING THE TERM WAY BACK WHEN I WAS A VERY YOUNG FELLOW, DURING THE FIRST RUN OF THE TV SHOW *THE BEVERLY HILL-BILLIES*. IT WAS THE TERM THE CLAMPETTS USED WHEN A YOUNG MAN WOULD TRY TO WIN THE AFFECTIONS OF ELLIE MAY. *COURTING* IS SOMETHING I DO A LOT EVEN NOW THAT I'M MARRIED. BARBARA AND I ARE STILL VERY INTENTIONAL ABOUT PURSUING EACH OTHER THROUGH CONTINUED COURTING—I TRY TO GIVE HER REASONS, EVERY DAY, TO KNOW THAT SHE MARRIED THE RIGHT GUY; AND SHE DOES THAT FOR ME TOO.

But what does courting have to do with diversity? Well, what makes a cool city? Is it the architecture? What makes a cool company? Is it the opportunities? Well, yes! Although none of that makes much of a difference if it is a community where beautiful public spaces are enjoyed by only one group of people, or exciting opportunities are offered to only a few. It is places of residence as well as places of business where people truly feel as if they belong that are the ones that thrive. The more diverse a community is, the smarter and more innovative it is too. In order to make a community that is not merely welcoming but also embracing, employees and residents need to be courted. They need to be given reasons, on a regular basis, to stay. They need to know that their contributions are appreciated and valued.

★ ★

When was the last time your downtown merchants threw a Customer Appreciation Day? Are managers at your company empowered to reward employees for a job well done? When was the last time you treated someone who works under you to coffee, just because he or she does a fine job on a day-to-day basis? When was the last time you went out of your way to make a new resident feel welcomed in your city? Bonus points if the new resident was different from you and/or the majority of other residents in your town!

Way
84
Heritage Tour

FOR SOME, A PLANTATION IS A SYMBOL OF THE GENTEEL SOUTH, A RELAXED AND LEISURELY WAY OF LIFE—BOUGAINVILLEA AND MINT JULIPS AND ALL. FOR OTHERS, A PLANTATION REPRESENTS ONE OF THE HARDEST AND MOST INHUMANE PERIODS OF AMERICAN HISTORY. THIS IS THE POWER OF WHAT I CALL "HERITAGE TOURS"—EXPERIENCING ONE SITE, SUCH AS A PLANTATION, WITH PEOPLE WHO WILL LIKELY HAVE VERY DIFFERENT REACTIONS TO ITS HISTORY.

You can organize a large bus tour or just go with a small group of friends, but in either case the point is to go to a site that is going to evoke different responses from different people. I used plantations as my example because they so powerfully fit the purpose, but there are others. Little Bighorn Battlefield in Montana, the Lower East Side Tenement Museum in New York City, even the statue of Nathan Bedford Forrest, from whom Tom Hank's character Forrest Gump was named, in Nashville, Tennessee, are all possibilities.

There are at least two sides to every story—go on vacation and experience both of them.

Take a road trip with people of a different ethnicity and experience different historically significant sites together. Discuss the events that took place there, both the good and the bad, and share perspectives. You might find the insights you give and receive will change a mind, or   a life.

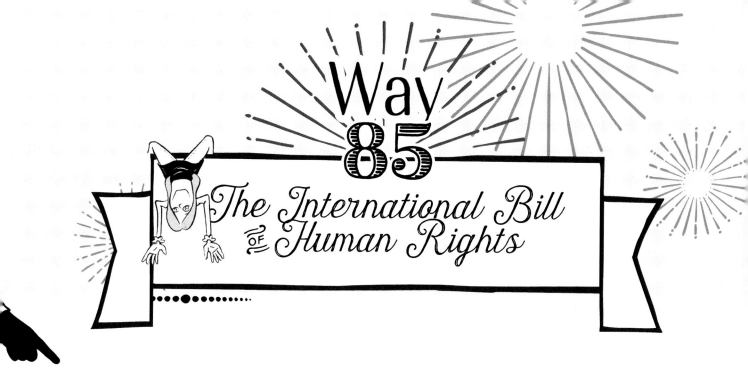

Way 85

The International Bill of Human Rights

THE UNITED NATIONS IS AN INTERNATIONAL ORGANIZATION FOUNDED IN 1945, AT A TIME WHEN MANY NATIONS IN THE WORLD LAY IN RUINS AND THEIR PEOPLE CRAVED PEACE AFTER LONG YEARS OF WAR. THE CHARTER OF THIS NOW-AUGUST ORGANIZATION WAS, AND IS, TO PROMOTE COOPERATION AMONG THE WORLD'S NATIONS—AND TO PREVENT THE FUTURE EVENT OF SUCH CATASTROPHIC WAR.

One of the first undertakings of this new organization was to create the Universal Declaration of Human Rights, the first global declaration of basic rights to which every human being on the planet is entitled. This document was adopted by the United Nations General Assembly in 1948 and it serves to this day as the standard by which the greatest portion of the world understands and protects fundamental, inherent human rights.

It's always important to appreciate where we've come from, and the foundational principles that guide us as we grow. Research the Universal Declaration of Human Rights; its origin and meaning. Become a part of a local organization that affirms this declaration. Here's a place to satart: www.un.org/en/universal-declaration-human-rights/index.html.

Way 86
Purchasing Power

$830 BILLION. COULD EVEN A SMALL PORTION OF THAT NUMBER BOOST YOUR BOTTOM LINE? I WOULD THINK SO! YET MANY COMPANIES DON'T KNOW THE FIRST THING ABOUT HOW TO REACH THE VERY SIGNIFICANT AND GROWING MARKET PORTION THAT THIS NUMBER REPRESENTS: THE LGBT COMMUNITY.

Reaching the LGBTQ market should be a part of the strategic marketing plan of any company that sells a product or service—or, in other words, pretty much every company out there. Here are some things you may not know about the LGBTQ market:

- 23% of this community have a higher median household income;
- 24% of this community have more than average equity in their homes;
- 26% of gay men say they will pay more for top quality brands;
- 30% of this community have taken a major vacation in the past year.

When was the last time your organization had a strategic conversation on reaching this influential market? Some companies struggle with going after this market, but others are working hard to etch their brands into the hearts of this affluent global community.

Get to know the LGBTQ market segment. Check out the National Gay & Lesbian chamber of commerce as your introduction: *www.nglcc.org.*

173

Way 87

Put the Cuffs on Hate

YOU MAY—OR MAY NOT—BE SURPRISED BY HOW MANY HATE CRIMES STILL HAPPEN.

There are organizations, such as the National Institute for Justice and the Southern Poverty Law Center, that track hate crime activity and can provide you with statistics for where your state stands in the ranking nationally. No matter how low your state may score, this will not be pleasant information to have, but it will be eye-opening to learn more about man's inhumanity to his fellow man.

For almost as far back as you can go into history, mankind has had a seemingly insatiable urge to abuse and mistreat each other. While the institution of slavery in the U.S. and the Jewish Holocaust are two of the largest, and more recent, examples of the mass perpetration of hate crimes—and while there are people around the globe who speak up with passion about these sort of heinous deeds—there are too many other people who choose to look the other way, or to offer lame excuses for criminal behavior, or to dismiss the idea of hate crimes as even real because if we don't see them on the news, we assume they aren't happening. Trust me, friend; they are.

This must be our bottom line: no one has any right whatsoever to harm another person simply because they are different. Period.

Ask your local police department or a legal professional on this matter to come to your school, your church, or your organization and give a presentation on hate crimes—what they are, why they happen, and what your part is to stop them.

Way 88
Tell it Like it T-I-IS

THERE'S A SAYING IN THE AFRICAN-AMERICAN COMMUNITY: TELL IT LIKE IT T-I-S – AND YOU'VE GOT TO SPELL IT OUT JUST THAT WAY AS YOU SAY IT. IT MEANS TO SPEAK TRUTH.

Why don't we tell it like it T-I-S more often?

Political correctness is the avoidance of expressions or actions that someone could perceive to be exclusive, or insulting to people or groups of people who have been historically disadvantaged, or have suffered from structural discrimination. In this context, what we're really talking about is basic human decency.

I've come to believe, however, that political correctness, taken to the extreme, does more to destroy substantive conversations than almost anything else.

One's ability to have the deeper dialogues has a lot to do with one's maturity and emotional intelligence. While it may produce temporary comfort to avoid hard conversations, it does not foster lasting peace.

There is a big difference between being politically correct and being a coward. All great changes in society started with a person or a group presenting a different opinion or way of thinking, regardless of the consequence that followed. Ask your uncomfortable questions, relate your own story with honesty, listen to your neighbor's story with real curiosity. As long as you do these things with respect, you'll always be smarter and more confident at the end of the conversation.

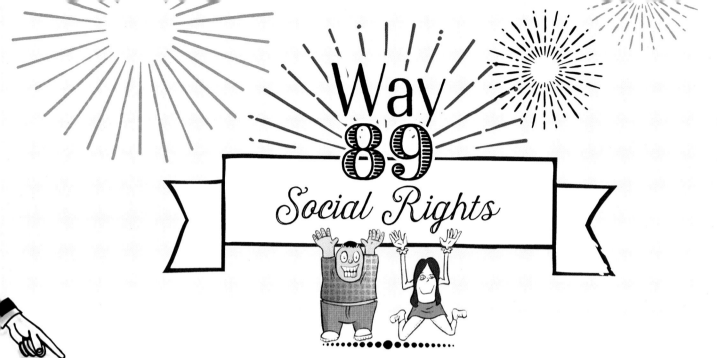

Way 89
Social Rights

DR. MARTIN LUTHER KING SAID: "INJUSTICE ANYWHERE IS A THREAT TO JUSTICE EVERYWHERE." THESE DAYS WE HAVE A FRONT-ROW SEAT TO INJUSTICE AS IT HAPPENS. SOMEONE IS SHOT BY THE POLICE—THE VIDEO IS UP ON YOUTUBE. SYRIAN REFUGEE CHILDREN ARE BATTLING IN FRIGID COLD FOR SURVIVAL—PHOTOS ARE THERE ON OUR FACEBOOK FEED.

Social media is a key player in not just documenting injustice but in relieving it. You live in Maine but you're outraged by a hate crime that has been perpetrated in New Mexico? Post news articles about it on your Facebook page to alert and involve your circle of friends. Want to bring attention to the plight of animals being used to test cosmetics? Sign a petition, or even start your own petition, through sites such as ge.org. Want to help the victims of flooding in Louisiana, b~

afford to take time off from your job in Wisconsin? Go th~

of relief organizations such as *redcross.org* and make a dor~

online.

~und Burke once said, "Nobody made a greater mistake than he w~

~ng because he could do only a little." These days, because of techr~

~he small things count and are amplified.

★ ★

Back in the 1970s, young, budding social activists were taught that to fully participate in democracy they should aim to write five snail-mail letters a week to the influential folks who could affect change. Here's a more modern challenge: send an e-mail to your congressional representative or senator, sign an online petition from an elected representative or social justice organization; post a news article about a cause that moves you to Twitter. Hint: make certain your articles are from reputable news organizations that fact-check content!

Way 90
Power To the People

SPEAKING OF OUR CONGRESSIONAL REPRESENTATIVES AS WE JUST DID IN WAY 89, DO YOU KNOW WHO YOURS ARE? AND DO YOU KNOW WHERE THEY STAND ON KEY ISSUES THAT ARE IMPORTANT TO YOU? SPECIFICALLY, DO YOU KNOW WHERE YOUR REPRESENTATIVES STAND ON THE ISSUE OF DIVERSITY AND INCLUSION AND, EVEN MORE, IF THEIR VOTING RECORD REFLECTS THEIR STANCE?

The truth is that many of our representatives don't have a documented stand on these issues, and that's mighty unfortunate because America, as well as the rest of the world, is changing its complexion. Leadership of the kind that's needed in the halls of Congress is more complex these days as one size no longer fits all. A person whose leadership philosophy doesn't incorporate the world's growing diversity in this day and age is sorely mistaken and out of touch.

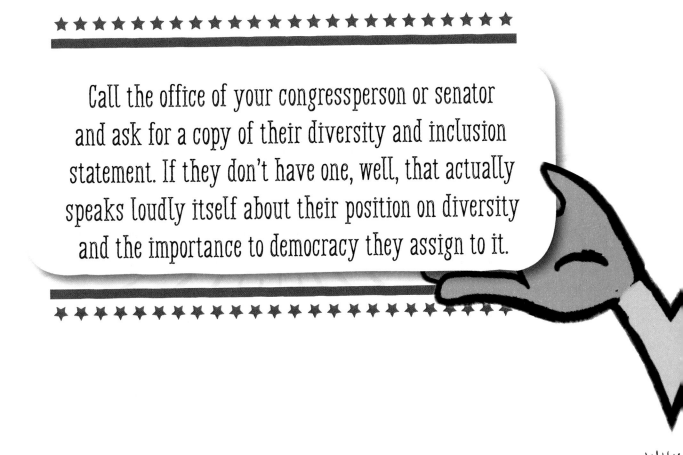

Call the office of your congressperson or senator and ask for a copy of their diversity and inclusion statement. If they don't have one, well, that actually speaks loudly itself about their position on diversity and the importance to democracy they assign to it.

Way 91
Across The Waters

AS A KID, MY TEACHER ASSIGNED EACH STUDENT A PEN PAL FROM ANOTHER COUNTRY. I WOULD EVER SO NEATLY WRITE MY LETTER, APPLY POSTAGE, AND MY TEACHER WOULD SEND IT. I ALWAYS WAS EXCITED AS I CAREFULLY TORE OPEN THE REPLY AIRMAIL ENVELOPE, EAGER TO READ ABOUT MY NEW FRIEND AND HIS LIFE IN A FARAWAY LAND.

I think having a pen pal at an early age is what started my enduring interest in cultures that were different from my own—interest no doubt solidified when I toured the world with Up With People (*upwithpeople.org*), an organization that has been using music to educate and inspire people while bridging cultural barriers, worldwide, for over fifty years.

These days, with social media and video chat apps, it's much easier to stay

…nected with people from all over the world. Our diets, accents, and la…
e and latitude are different, but it's fair to say it's still surprising how v…
ch we all have in common with each other.

★ ★

Connect with someone across the waters. And do you know the best place to start? Social media. Facebook, LinkedIn, Twitter, Instagram—these contemporary ways of communicating with each other are great for staying in touch with your existing circle, but they are also amazing ways to connect with people from all over the globe. Join a group or two on Facebook that is in line with your interests—a community that supports a cause you care about, or reads and reviews a genre of literature that you like to read. Read the group's newsfeed and contribute to it yourself—ask questions, provide answers. Start your friendship through common interests on social media and, who knows, one of you may someday get on a plane so you can meet each other in person.

Way
92
Press The Issue

NEWS ORGANIZATIONS ARE, THESE DAYS, COVERING TOPICS SUCH AS RACE, GENDER, AND EVEN AGE DISCRIMINATION WITH MORE VIGOR THAN THEY EVER HAVE IN THE PAST. I'M GLAD THEY'RE DOING IT, BUT THEY'RE NOT DOING IT OUT OF ALTRUISM—THEY'RE DOING IT BECAUSE THEY KNOW THESE ARE SUBJECTS THAT ARE OF INTEREST TO THEIR READERS. AND THEIR READERS ARE INTERESTED BECAUSE AS THE NATION IS BECOMING MORE DIVERSE, SO DOES READERSHIP.

I'm here to advocate for a different kind of coverage of race and gender and aging. Rather than covering these sorts of topics in a one-dimensional way, as issues to be dealt with or problems to be solved, I'd like to see them covered as opportunities, competitive advantages to be realized. There is so much that's good coming from a more diverse pool—more and different talents, ideas and inventions and innovation—that it's a shame to see the whole of diversity pigeon-holed into a problem.

★ ★

If your local news outlet doesn't already cover diversity from a positive perspective, encourage them to do so. What would a regular, ongoing column or blog dedicated to diversity trends in your community look like? How would it highlight the vibrancy of your local and regional ethnic mix? How would it positively impact your surrounding business community, neighborhood communities, and potential for tourism? What would happen if your community became known as a place of belonging for every color and creed? Maybe you could even volunteer to write the amazing column or blog yourself!

★ ★

Way 93

Calling All Colors

THE CULTURE OF CONNECTION THAT THE RISING GENERATION POSSESSES IS AS ECLECTIC AND DIVERSE AS ANYTHING I'VE EVER SEEN. AS I'VE ALREADY MENTIONED, THE SCHOOL DISTRICT IN WHICH MY WIFE AND I RAISED OUR CHILDREN HAS OVER SEVENTY LANGUAGES SPOKEN AMONG STUDENTS REPRESENTING SOME SIXTY-EIGHT COUNTRIES. THIS IS THE MAGNIFICENTLY DIVERSE PUBLIC SCHOOL SYSTEM OF KENTWOOD IN MICHIGAN, AND IT MAY WELL BE AN EXTREME EXAMPLE OF DIVERSITY AT ITS BEST, BUT IT REALLY IS JUST ONE EXAMPLE OF THE SORT OF EVERYDAY DIVERSITY OUR KIDS EXPERIENCE AS AMERICA CHANGES DEMOGRAPHICALLY.

I have found that the more multicultural the environment in which they grow up, the more culturally competent, thoughtful, and comfortable our kids are. This is exciting to me because I have traveled around the globe working for Fortune 500 companies and I know the type of marketplace that will welcome our youth. I can tell you two things that that this marketplace is definitely not: monolithic and homogeneous. Those parents that both understand and embrace that reality will be the ones who properly prepare their kids to succeed and contribute in the 21st-century global marketplace.

One organization that is extremely valuable in helping prepare kids for the ever more multicultural marketplace is Calling All Colors. It's an organization that assembles area youth to have cross-cultural, multi-ethnic dialogue that works to uproot stereotypes, prejudice, and bias. This energetic, bright-eyed, intellectually curious group is a force to be reckoned with. They are adept and fearless when it comes to the new world that is forming around them. Let's do our part as adults to not burden their shoulders with the baggage that we carry.

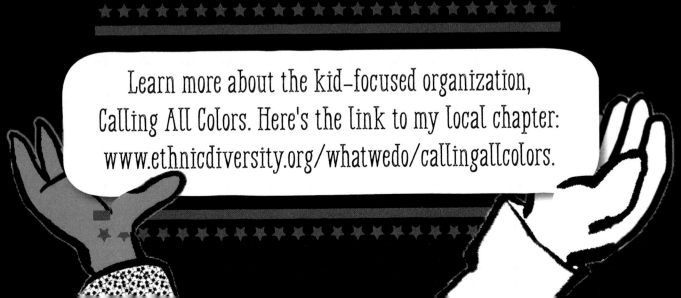

Learn more about the kid-focused organization, Calling All Colors. Here's the link to my local chapter: www.ethnicdiversity.org/whatwedo/callingallcolors.

Way 94

In-site

WITH ALL THE MARKET DATA, CENSUS DATA, DATA ON THE MULTI-CULTURAL ECONOMY—WELL, THE BUSINESS CASE FOR WHY HOMOGENEOUS MARKETING COLLATERAL LOOKS PAINFULLY DATED IS A NO BRAINER. THE MARKETPLACE IS MORE RESPONSIVE THAN EVER. COMPANIES THAT CONNECT WITH THEIR CUSTOMERS, WHO SEE THEMSELVES MORE AS A MOVEMENT THAN SIMPLY A BRAND, ARE THE ONES WHO WIN. THOSE ORGANIZATIONS THAT STILL THINK WHAT USED TO WORK WILL CONTINUE TO WORK IN THE NEW DEMOGRAPHY WILL BE PENALIZED SWIFTLY AND DEEPLY.

Seeing a homogeneous website or commercial these days says a lot about the organization that is behind it—and the biggest thing it says is that this organization is out of touch with the pulse of the marketplace. The world in which we live and work is increasingly diverse and it is critical for current and future customers to see themselves in your web, TV, and print strategy. And, to be honest with you, it just looks more interesting.

When I do see an advertisement or a web site that gets it right, I take the time to write a letter or make a call and commend the marketing department for making that choice. And when I see a company get it wrong, I'll speak up too, although I often get a rote and rehearsed reply. In those cases, I just shrug; I guess their competitor(s) will have to enjoy the increased market share.

★ ★

Look at your company's website and other advertising to see if your current or potential customers can vicariously see themselves represented. If not, communicate that to your organization's marketing department and suggest a more inclusive look.

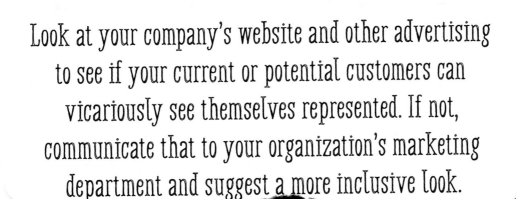

Way 95
Go Global

THE UNDERGROUND RAILROAD FREEDOM CENTER IN CINCINNATI, OHIO, IS ONE OF THE NATIONAL TREASURES OF OUR NATION. MY ORIGINAL INTENT IN GOING THERE FOR THE FIRST TIME WAS TO LEARN MORE ABOUT THE IMPORTATION OF AFRICANS AND THE U.S. DOMESTIC SLAVE TRADE. THIS THEY COVERED IN SOME OF THE MOST INTERESTING WAYS—BUT THAT WAS NOT WHERE THEY STOPPED. ON THE CONTRARY, THIS WAS WHERE IT BEGAN. THE EXTENSIVE AMOUNT OF TIME, RESEARCH, STUDY, AND HEART THAT WAS PUT INTO THIS MUSEUM IS BREATHTAKING. AS YOU WALK THROUGH THE VARIOUS PARTS OF THE CENTER, YOU ARE COMPLETELY IMMERSED IN THE HISTORY OF THE SLAVE TRADE—AND YOU ARE REMINDED OF HOW VERY RECENTLY, IN THE SCOPE OF WORLD HISTORY, THE AMERICAN SLAVE TRADE ACTUALLY HAPPENED.

I was also very impressed to see that our white brothers and sisters were represented in this space, and touched to see the part some of them played, even giving their own lives, as they stood alongside African-Americans and spoke out about the injustices, regardless of the consequences.

Possibly the most amazing part of the experience was the Freedom Center component, where attention is focused on global unrest and the continuing cry for freedom around the world. Brothers and sisters, oppression is oppression and freedom is freedom, in all lands, and all times.

Check out the Freedom Center's website, www.freedomcenter.org, and plan a trip to see this amazing place for yourself. Research issues of civil unrest globally that have polarized—and continue to polarize—various communities within those countries.

Way 96
The Big League

WHILE IT TAKES A VILLAGE TO RAISE A CHILD, IT TAKES MANY PASSIONATE PEOPLE TO BUILD THE VILLAGE IN WHICH TO RAISE THAT CHILD. THE VILLAGE, IN TURN, REQUIRES STAUNCH DEFENDERS, ORGANIZATIONS OF PEOPLE DEVOTED TO MAKING AND KEEPING THE VILLAGE SAFE. COLLECTIVELY, THESE ORGANIZATIONS SHAPE OUR SOCIETY, MANY TIMES BY STANDING IN HARM'S WAY AND REFUSING TO COMPROMISE WITH THOSE WHO WOULD DESTROY THE COMMUNITY.

An important village-building organization in our larger community is the Anti-Defamation League. Founded in 1913 "to stop the defamation of the Jewish people and to secure justice and fair treatment to all," the ADL is tireless in their advocacy, and steadfast in their mission to make the world better for everyone. I truly believe it is organizations like this that, in their seemingly "behind the scenes" presence, wield an incredibly big hammer against bigotry, hate and other forms of prejudice. I hope you've taken from these pages that I am a strong proponent for action and not simply talk. Well, the ADL is an organization made up of people who have their sleeves rolled up and are not afraid to get in a scuffle or two. If this sounds like your kind of people, you should call them up and see how you can help them in their mission to secure justice and fair treatment for everyone.

Thank you ADL—you are making a difference for all of us.

Spend time on the website for the Anti-Defamation League, *www.adl.org*, to learn about their focus, mission and passion.

Way 97
Lend a Hand

IF YOU ARE LIKE ME, YOU LACK THE HANDYMAN GENE; I DO LIGHTBULB REPLACEMENT AND THAT'S ABOUT AS HANDY AS I GET. IF THIS IS ALSO AS FAR AS YOUR BUILDING SKILLS GO, YOU MAY SHY AWAY FROM VOLUNTEER OPPORTUNITIES THAT REQUIRE YOU TO... WELL, ACTUALLY BUILD SOMETHING. I FELT THE SAME WAY—BELIEVING THAT THE ONLY THING I WOULD BE ABLE TO DO IN THAT TYPE OF VOLUNTEERISM IS GET IN THE WAY. AND THEN I HAD THE OPPORTUNITY TO SPEND SOME TIME WITH MY LOCAL CHAPTER OF HABITAT FOR HUMANITY.

Having a home that one can call his or her own is life affirming, and Habit for Humanity has affirmed more lives than you could shake a hammer at. I had long wanted to lend my support to the organization, but my disability with hammer and nails and saws and screws had kept me away. But then my wife and her chapter of Jack and Jill of America had volunteered for a Habitat for Humanity project, so I went along.

The experienced project manager knew just what to do with me. I ended up painting boards that would form part of the exterior of the new home—valuable work that was necessary to the finished home, that exactly fit my skill level, and that made me feel integral to the whole honorable project.

Maybe you wouldn't be able to build a whole house, but, like me, you can probably wield a paintbrush, hammer nails into a board, or push a broom to clean up. In giving a few hours of labor, you will make a difference to a deserving family; and, in doing so, you just might change lives—theirs, and your own.

Become a volunteer for Habitat for Humanity, *www.habitat.org*, and be a part of building a dream for a deserving family.

Way 98
Wear the Message

SOME GREAT MESSAGES ARE SHOWING UP IN SOME OF THE MOST UNIQUE PLACES, THANKS IN GREAT PART TO OUR NEW-FOUND DIGITAL SAVVY. BUT I WONDER IF WE'RE OVERLOOKING A TERRIFIC MEDIUM FOR OUR MESSAGE, ONE THAT IS HIDDEN IN PLAIN SIGHT: THE NATIONAL COSTUME, THE UBIQUITOUS, HUMBLE T-SHIRT.

Think of the T-shirt as a cotton canvas for wearable art—and wearable advocacy. How would the slogan "Celebrate Diversity!" look with your company's logo on T-shirts at the next company party? Or what about "We Need Diverse Books!" on some T-shirts you sell to raise funds for your local public library?

Other benefits of T-shirts? The older they get, the more comfortable they become. And they're generally inexpensive to produce too, so selling your powerful pieces of art could be one way to fund a project or two for your organization.

Finally, don't forget, nearly everybody you'll ever meet wears them, even if it's just to relax on weekends or when they're working out, so you've got a ready-made customer base!

★ ★

Work with a local company or a local school to create a T-shirt with a diversity message. Sell the shirts and use the money to fund an ongoing diversity education program at the school.

Way 99

WOKE

and How to Stay That Way

SPIKE LEE IS A FILM DIRECTOR AND MASTER STORYTELLER. IN HIS MOVIE *SCHOOL DAZE*, AFTER MUCH STRIFE AND UPHEAVAL ON A FICTITIOUS HBCU (HISTORICALLY BLACK COLLEGE/UNIVERSITY) CAMPUS, ONE OF THE CHARACTERS YELLS, "WAKE UP! WAKE UP!"

In contemporary culture, being woke means being aware of what is going on in your community, especially in terms of racial and social justice. It is hard to be woke. That's because it's part of the human experience to be more comfortable with the routine—the same route to work, the same dinner on Tuesday night, the same friends who think just like you do talking about the same things. These are just a few examples of the sorts of ruts that slowly lull one to sleep. In the past, people lived in homogeneous communities; the larger

—heck, even the closest village—was cut off because it was diffi[cult to comm]unicate with, let alone visit. Falling into a rut and living out your [life] the monotonous way others around you were living out their live[s may have] been acceptable, or even a good way of coping with a hard exis[tence. These] days, however, you sleep at your own peril.

How does one stay woke? Well, one way for sure is to spend tim[e with peopl]e who are different from you, and who think differently from you[. You can'] t stay woke in isolation; it takes community to keep us on our t[oes, to ground our] intentionality.

★ ★

Lean into your relationships. Bring different people around your dinner table and into your conversation. Discuss, learn, teach, disagree—even argue—but do so with an open mind: everyone's experience of the world is different, and you owe it to yourself, if not to your neighbors, to at least entertain the notion that someone who disagrees with you may have a valid point or two. Remember, the magic is outside of your comfort zone, not in it.

Way 100
Work It!

TALK TO ALMOST ANY PERSON IN AMERICA TODAY ABOUT THEIR FAMILY HERITAGE AND YOU'LL LIKELY FIND VERY FEW PEOPLE WHO WON'T BE A HYPHENATE, OR EVEN A MULTIPLE HYPHENATE: AFRICAN-IRISH, ITALIAN-POLISH, CREOLE-WELSH-CHOCTAW. IN ORDER TO PROPERLY CELEBRATE OUR DIVERSITY, IT'S IMPORTANT WE EACH START BY CELEBRATING THE PRIDE WE TAKE IN THE CULTURES WE OR OUR ANCESTORS CAME FROM. I FIND, HOWEVER, THAT WITH EACH SUCCESSIVE GENERATION, WE GROW MORE DISTANT FROM OUR ROOTS. OUR GRANDPARENTS' OR GREAT-GRANDPARENTS' IMMIGRANT STORIES ARE LOST TO OUR YOUNG PEOPLE, JUST AS GREAT-GRANDMA'S RECIPE FOR HER AWARD-WINNING BLUEBERRY PIE IS BUT A DELICIOUS MEMORY TO OUR ELDERLY AUNTS AND UNCLES.

Amidst those bits of intriguing, and often important, information that can be lost among the generations is the work our families engaged in to sustain themselves—and, ultimately, us—along the way. Did your great-great-grandfather work on the railroads, making travel easier from sea to shining sea? Did an ancestor have a part in building the Empire State Building, the Golden Gate Bridge, the Hoover Dam, the White House? Did they mine the coal that warmed our homes or did they harvest the fields that fed us at our tables? Was your grandmother or great-grandmother one of the more than 80% of immigrant women who took up the needle trades and literally stitched together the fabric of our nation? The great and small works of our nation were built by hands of all colors, from all corners of the earth.

One of the best times to tell family stories is after dinner, gathered at the table, well-fed, with perhaps an extra cup of coffee or a second piece of pie. By all means, give your young people the advantage of being able to point with pride at your family's contribution to the creation of the world in which we all live.

Way 101
Your Way

WELL, MY FRIEND, THIS BOOK IS CALLED 101 WAYS TO ENJOY THE MOSAIC, BUT THAT'S ONLY BECAUSE THIS IS MY LAST WAY, NOT YOUR LAST WAY.

We are so much more complete as a community when we're able to learn from each other, so teach me—teach us—the way or ways in which you believe we can evolve into a more diverse, inclusive, and perfect society. When you've created your way—when you've thought of something you'd like to do, or have put into practice a way that the rest of us haven't even dreamed about yet—I'd be very pleased if you'd share it at the 101 Ways Community page at *www.101waystoenjoythemosaic.com*. Together, let's turn my modest 101 Ways into 1001 Ways, even 10,001 Ways!

Thank you for coming along on this journey so far. I look forward to continuing to walk together.

_____

_____

_____

_____

_____

_____

_____

_____

_____

Acknowledgments

To Mom (Ruth Jones-Hairston), Educator Extraordinaire: Your support, wisdom and unconditional love have always motivated me to go for it and to never forget that a life truly lived is a life given to the service of others. From Korea, to Blue Lake, to Up With People, you allowed the world to be my classroom, which has everything to do with the writing of this book.

To the amazing clients of Global Bridgebuilders: Thank you for always giving me a place at the table to advise, to teach, sometimes to challenge and always to learn. You are the best and you make me better everyday!

To Bill Harris: We have over thirty years of history, my friend. I'm so very grateful to have you in my life. Thanks for helping to organize the manuscript in a way that made sense. You are an incredible craftsman of the written word and I celebrate you.

To Andrea Hoffman: I'm so glad that Barbara saw the commonality at

Carnegie Hall and made sure we connected. I very much appreciate our friendship—you rock, Red!

To Michael Hyter: Thank you for the foreword but more importantly, your friendship. So glad that we met—you're a great brother.

To Lynn Vannucci: Thank you for seeing the value in the manuscript and being the champion to get it to market. You're a great advocate and listener.

To Joel Brooks: Thanks Pastor Joel for being a constant friend and source of wisdom. I'm a better father, husband, brother, son and man because of you.

And finally to all Diversity and Inclusion Professionals: Your efforts are not in vain. I applaud you for the work you do to make organizations and communities around the world better. Keep saying it, keep teaching it, and keep living it. You are an amazing community!

About the author

101 Ways to Enjoy the Mosaic has been created from Skot Welch's thirty-year experience in international business and diversity and inclusion consulting. He has pioneered diversity and inclusion initiatives for Fortune 500 firms in Asia, Europe, Africa, and South America. Today, he is the owner of a successful innovation-through-inclusion firm, Global Bridgebuilders, which is focused on building sustainable, ROI-oriented frameworks that support cultural competence for organizations in a broad range of industries. Skot has found that embracing our differences expands our capacities whether in business, in our communities, and especially in our lives.

Uptown Professional Press is an imprint of Water Street Press, in partnership with Uptown Ventures Group, publishing books that focus on diversity issues and progressive politics. Look for other UPP titles, including *A Black Man in the White House: Barack Obama and the Triggering of America's Racial-Aversion Crisis* by Cornell Belcher.

www.waterstreetpressbooks.com